The Coming Post-Christian Tsunami

*Connecting with an increasingly
unchurched culture*

JON PERRIN

DEDICATION

To Robin: Anyone that knows you realizes that without you I am hopelessly lost. You are more than just my wife… you are truly my best friend. Your fierce loyalty, patient love and unwavering support have made me the man I am today. This has been quite a journey. I am so thankful that you've taken it with me. I love doing life with you.

To Ryan, Ashton and Emma.: You have taught me more about life, love and character than any mentor ever could. I am proud to be your dad.

CONTENTS

Introduction   1

SECTION 1

Chapter 1
Our Story (In A Nutshell)   13

Chapter 2
The Winds Of Change   19

Chapter 3
The Next Generations   27

Chapter 4
A Radical Approach   36

Chapter 5
What To Expect   40

SECTION 2

AUTHENTICITY   44

Chapter 6
Just Be Real!   45

Chapter 7
The Power Of Vulnerability   52

AIM   60

Chapter 8
Your Church's DNA   61

Chapter 9
Who Am I?   69

Chapter 10
Why Churches Fail   77

ACCESSIBILITY   83

Chapter 11
What A Church Should Look Like   84

Chapter 12
Entry Level Ministry   102

Chapter 13
Preaching The Gospel In A Post-Christian Context   108

ALIGNMENT   120

Chapter 14
Leading Younger Generations   121

Chapter 15
Vision Casting   127

Chapter 16
Developing Your Leadership Team   138

Chapter 17
Finding Your Elisha   151

Chapter 18
Everything Counts   159

ACTION   167

Chapter 19
Going Beyond Your Church Walls   168

Chapter 20
Sharing Your Faith With The Unchurched   174

AVAILABILITY   184

Chapter 21
True Community   185

Chapter 22
Biblical Small Groups   193

SECTION 3

Chapter 23
Where The Rubber Meets The Road   200

Chapter 24
Finish Strong   210

Appendix   218

About The Author   221

Bibliography   222

ACKNOWLEDGMENTS

This book would not be possible without the support, encouragement and strategic insight of my wife, Robin. I would also like to thank the many leaders that have invested in me along the way, especially my pastor, Dr. Gerald Brooks.

Introduction

A Tsunami Warning System

On December 26, 2004 at 7:58am a massive earthquake ripped a 750-mile gash in the seafloor northwest of Sumatra. Measuring a magnitude of 9.1, it released an amount of energy equivalent to approximately 550 million times the atomic bomb dropped on Hiroshima in 1945[1]

The damage from the earthquake in Sumatra was compounded by a series of four gigantic waves – some reportedly 80 - 100 feet tall and traveling at speeds upwards of 500 mph – that smashed into the shore. In many places the waves traveled over a mile inland.[2]

People near the epicenter only had about five minutes to react. In several areas the sea withdrew from the shoreline, causing many curious children and onlookers to wander out onto the exposed seafloor. After the waves hit, those that survived the incoming surge of water were now in danger of being swept out to sea by the receding waters.[3]

Within two hours the waves hit the unsuspecting coastal areas of Thailand, India and Sri Lanka. All told, a quarter of a million people lost their lives. And more than 1.7 million were displaced, trying to survive long enough to make it to the refugee camps set up by various organizations.[4]

The lack of a tsunami warning system caused an even greater loss of life. Although in Indonesia very little could have been done to prevent the catastrophic loss of life because they had only minutes to find higher ground, it is estimated that at least 60,000 people in other countries could have been saved if there was some sort of a warning system in place.[5]

While nothing can compare with the loss of so many lives, there are striking similarities between this event and the current spiritual condition in North America. Inasmuch as the 2004 Indian Ocean Tsunami brought physical destruction, the coming Post-Christian Tsunami will bring devastating spiritual consequences.

Many churches are still trying to survive the effects of the postmodern earthquake. The violent shaking caught them by surprise. The cultural landscape changed dramatically as many familiar "landmarks" were reduced to rubble. Countless pastors are still trying to pick up the pieces after last cultural shift caught them unprepared. Their struggling churches are aging; and other than a sovereign move of God, there isn't much hope. They have no clue that something even worse is coming. A cultural tsunami is already upon us – Post-Christianity. The water on the shoreline is receding and the wave is getting ready to come crashing in. It threatens to produce even more catastrophic damage than postmodernism for those that aren't ready.

We feel an urgency to sound a clarion call to spiritual leaders in North America. Having served in Europe for more than a decade, we have seen the future of American churches, should they maintain their current course. It is our hope that this book will serve as a cultural tsunami warning system that pastors and church leaders will heed.

The Situation On The Ground

> *The Israelites served the LORD throughout the lifetime of Joshua and the leaders who outlived him – those who had seen all the great things the LORD had done for Israel...*
>
> *After that generation died another generation grew up that did not acknowledge the LORD or remember the mighty things he had done for Israel."*

Judges 2:7, 10

Unfortunately, this describes the situation on the ground in Europe. Although culturally 85% of the population is connected to Christianity, according to the European Spiritual Estimate less than 2% of the population has a genuine relationship with Christ. The current populace is second to fifth generation unchurched. Over the centuries "Christianity" devolved from a life-changing connection with our Creator into a works-based means of power. Guilt, shame and the fear of hell were wielded quite effectively as powerful weapons to manipulate, control and pilfer entire populations.

As people realized what was really happening they abandoned their faith (and religion) altogether. This led to a self-centered worldview. After all, if God doesn't exist there is no reason to consider someone else, or to be generous and kind. A me-first culture ends up draining the spiritual and emotional life from its people.

This is EXACTLY what we are now seeing in American culture as well. Our amazing nation that began with the free pursuit of God has wandered far from Him. For the past few election cycles, civic and religious leaders have sought to use religion to garner support and votes. But just as Europeans weren't stupid, neither are Americans. They can see through the hype to the real motivation behind this push for the hearts of religious people. And they're fed up with it!

The American Church has sadly become a powerless, and sometimes oblivious, bystander to the events unfolding around it. It has lost its edge. Rather than engage and influence the culture around it, the American Church has, by and large, buried its head in the sand.

We HAVE To Grow!

Pastors need to be aware that the skills and knowledge that got them this far may not be enough for them to lead their churches into the future. My initial university major was in computer science. One of the things our professors told us over and over again was that by the time we received our degree much of what we learned would be obsolete. We would have to continually keep learning. We couldn't plan on simply graduating, getting an easy job and settling in for a nice, quiet career.

We've learned that this concept also applies to ministry. Shortly after we graduated from Bible school some of the practical training we received was already outdated, especially concerning legal issues. The world around us is changing rapidly, at a faster rate than at any time in history. We have to continually be learning and adapting. I realize this is scary and threatening for some pastors. But if you will trust the Holy Spirit (Jesus called Him "the Teacher") and be willing to learn, grow and change, the sky is the limit! Change is painful... no doubt about it. But it's the only way to engage a rapidly evolving world.

Some pastors will respond, "My church is doing just fine. We're not a trendy church, so this probably won't affect us." During the reigns of the biblical King Ahab and King Solomon everything looked great on the outside, too. Israel was experiencing a time of financial prosperity, political stability and peace with their enemies. But below the waterline things were falling apart.

King Ahab led the people away from their God into worshipping the gods of the neighboring countries, especially those of his wife, Jezebel, a Phoenician princess. The people willingly followed because their lives were comfortable. But they were wandering farther and farther away from God.

King Solomon was the wisest and most prosperous king ever to rule Israel because he began his reign by pursuing the God of Israel with all his heart. But 1 Kings 11:4 informs us that as he grew older he began to worship foreign gods in order to appease his foreign wives. The rest of the chapter reveals the results of his kingdom's inner moral decay. Only days after his death his glorious kingdom split in two.

We are, of course, not implying that pastors are succumbing to moral impropriety. We are saying, however, that although things may be going well now, the coming cultural shift will make it increasingly more difficult to do ministry, even among the older generations. Just because your church doesn't seem to be affected now doesn't mean that you will be able to maintain the status quo. Your efforts will only produce diminishing returns.

I don't mean to be a doomsday prophet, but we've seen the future and it isn't pretty. If you refuse to change, your days as a leader are numbered and your church will die. This is true for any organization, whether sacred or secular. Jack Welch, former CEO of General Electric, often says, "If the rate of change inside an institution is less than the rate of change outside, the end is in sight." While there may not be an expiration date on the vision God gave you for your church, there is always an expiration date on the programs and strategy. What worked in the 70s, 80s and 90s will, for the most part, not prove very effective anymore. And what's working now won't be very effective in 10 - 20 years because the culture will morph into something else.

Avoid THEM At All Costs!

In the early days of the Church the followers of this burgeoning movement experienced strong persecution. The believers didn't know what was coming next, but they knew the life-changing message of the Gospel needed to be shared wherever they went. And that is precisely what they did![6] They weren't able to remain in Jerusalem so they scattered and took the message with them just as Jesus had instructed His disciples to do.[7] This was the first major missional movement… and it was wildly successful! Why? Because the believers adapted to engage their environment. They played the hand that they were dealt.

When I was a teenager my youth pastor taught me to avoid people that didn't believe like I did. *They* would bring me down. *They* would tempt me to abandon my faith. *They* would cause me to lose my heart for God. I was never to hang out with *them*! So I spent at least 4 days/nights per week at the church. I hung out with my Christian friends. I went to a Christian school. I bought books from a Christian bookstore. I did business with Christian businessmen and women. I did everything a good Christian should do. And in my eagerness to please God by separating myself from the world, I lost *all* connection with people that were far from God.

This is absolutely the opposite of what was written about Jesus by the people that walked with Him for three and a half years. These men observed that He seemed absolutely at home with people who were far from God.[8] Actually He seemed to *prefer* their company to that of the religious leaders. And these same "sinners" obviously felt safe with Him.[9] Jesus was apparently the life of the party.

It's time we got back to representing Jesus' grace-filled heart to a world that is in desperate need of Him! His biographers quoted Him as saying that He "came to seek and save the lost"[10] – people that are far from God! How can His followers do any less? And we can't do this from a distance. For the most part, in the USA the days of the tent crusades are over. But people will almost always respond to someone willing to invest in a relationship with them, someone who will actually *listen* to them instead of just trying to *preach* to (or at) them. People that are far from God need to feel safe, not just that they are the targets of someone's evangelistic efforts.

We definitely don't have all the answers, but there are some things we've learned over the years. As missionaries to secular Europe we observed some things that can help American churches connect with a world that is becoming increasingly oblivious – even hostile – to church and the Gospel. America's movers and shakers routinely tout the benefits of European culture. Our culture is drifting away from its spiritual roots toward the European secular model.

This book is the culmination of over 25 years of ministry, 13 of these years in Post-Christian (secular) Europe. We feel God has given us a message that the North American Church needs to hear, and a mandate to share it. Thankfully there are others that carry the same message. Our prayer is that church leaders would start to pay attention.

We believe that the local church is God's chosen tool for reaching the world. We are passionate about reaching a world full of people that are far from God… and most of these people have no clue that He desires a relationship with them! That said, if you truly want to reach the unchurched in a Post-Christian context, this book is a great place to start.

Following The Rules

As the Greek philosopher Heraclitus wisely said in 500 B.C., "Change is the only constant in life." We can either fight against it, let it drag us along while we whine or do our best to read the signs, anticipating how we need to adjust to face the coming challenges. If we choose the latter we have the best chance of not only surviving the changes, but actually thriving in the midst of them.

In 1984 MTV aired its first video – *Video Killed The Radio Star* by The Buggles. This song was truly prophetic in that MTV radically changed the way people experience popular music. The changes we're writing about in this book threaten to do the same to our churches.

The questions we're trying to answer are, *"What will kill the church in the coming decades if we don't adjust and engage the culture around us?"* and, *"How can our churches adapt in order to connect with a society that is running away from God?"* There is still time to change the trajectory of the American Church, but there is much work to be done!

We've heard the argument, "A church is a *church*… it's supposed to be *churchy*. Why would we change it to make it look like something it's not?" While I do understand where they're coming from, I believe this is flawed logic.

This is the same conversation the Early Church struggled with. In Acts 15, the hardline Jews claimed that the Gentiles had to first become Jewish by being circumcised, and then keep the Jewish Law in order to become Christians. After all, they reasoned, Jesus was the *Jewish* Savior. For Gentile men this brought PHYSICAL consequences. You had to REALLY want to be a Christian in order to join them!

Paul argued that to make it hard for people to become a part of the community of Christ-followers was counterproductive. Even the Jews couldn't keep all of their own rules! It became such a flashpoint that it threatened to split the burgeoning Church wide-open.

This was the reason for what we know as the Council at Jerusalem, found in Acts 15. All the Apostles and elders of the Church gathered to discuss the matter. Both the hardliners and Paul and Barnabas (who were joined by Peter) shared their respective points of view. What was the leaders' decision?

> *We should not make it difficult for the Gentiles who are turning to God.*

Acts 15:19

Did you catch that? They concluded that Christianity was a *heart* matter, not one of external rule following. They ended up asking the Gentiles to obey a few basic moral rules, and then invited them into their fellowship.

The Apostle Paul obviously felt it was his obligation to connect with people on their level. He believed we shouldn't force people to adapt to our customs and our style. He concluded that it is our responsibility to adapt the message to the culture of the people we are trying to reach. He wrote:

> Though I am free and belong to no one, I have made myself a slave to everyone, to win as many as possible… I have become all things to all people so that by all possible means I might save some.

> 1 Corinthians 9:19, 22

From 382 - 384 AD Jerome translated the Hebrew Bible into what we know as the Latin Vulgate, or, "Common Bible." He sought to bring the Gospel into the language of the common people, as did Martin Luther and so many others with their translations of the Bible.

This is *exactly* what we are suggesting – that we should contextualize the Gospel by using the language and idioms of today's common people. Or to put it another way, we need to adapt the style of our churches to actually reach the people that need to be reached.

We would never suggest that pastors change the *message*; only the *method*. Churches have the most important message in the world, but are doing a poor job of conveying it to a world that so desperately needs to hear it. Far too many churches (Baptist, Methodist, Assemblies of God, "Spirit-led" and Hipster churches) are the way they are because it's all their pastors know. Or maybe it's because the church leadership saw a certain style of ministry in a large, successful church with a highly gifted or charismatic pastor. No one is lining up to copy the style of a small, struggling church, even if there is evidence that God is at work among them.

We don't want to belittle people that see the world differently than we do. That would be stupid! We are all on the same team and want the same things. There's too little time to fight among ourselves over style issues. It's absolutely okay that a church is the way it is, as long as its leaders are following what God is actually telling them. We need to be celebrating these differences, not quarreling over them.

There are many great churches that have a style considerably different from the one we prefer. Although we grew up in

Charismatic/Word of Faith churches, we prefer a more up-to-date style of service. We, personally, consider most "contemporary" services to be old school. But preferences are simply *style* issues. We want to focus on *substance* issues.

Opportunities Abound

We encourage you to prayerfully read through this book and allow God to speak to your heart, revealing areas of your life and your church that need adjustment. Of course we understand not everyone will agree with what we've written. This is absolutely okay! As our spiritual father used to say, "Even an old cow knows how to eat the hay and spit out the sticks. Certainly you're at least as smart as an old cow." Our prayer is that our observations would produce healthy conversations concerning the future of the American Church.

This book is designed to be a catalyst that can help church leaders more precisely define exactly who/what God has created them and their churches to be. The discussion questions at the end of each section have been provided to help leaders summarize their thoughts and mentor their teams.

Because of our passion for church planting, many of the lessons will focus on things church planters need to know in order to effectively reach a Post-Christian audience. We believe that church planting is the most effective form of evangelism in today's world. But any leader with a heart set on learning will be able to understand and apply these principles to their setting. Jesus called this having "ears that hear."

Please understand that this isn't about making our churches cool or "hip." We aren't trying to update the message of the Gospel. We aren't suggesting that pastors go out and buy a pair of skinny jeans (PLEASE DON'T!!!), install fog machines and intelligent lighting, get a tattoo or a "Fauxhawk." We're all for innovation, but these are only external bells and whistles that don't impress a media-saturated generation. They have nothing to do with the actual *culture* of a church… and today's young adults can see right through them!

We *are* instead encouraging pastors to examine what their churches are doing and evaluate that against the what we've experienced in Post-Christian Europe. It is quite possible that some changes need to be made. We aren't throwing out the old ways simply because they are old. Even Solomon warned about this in Proverbs 22:28: "Do not move an ancient boundary stone set up by your ancestors." We are simply repackaging God's timeless truths to spark the interest of an increasingly godless society. As we said, the message doesn't change; only the method.

We understand that many who share our spiritual roots may consider this book to be unspiritual or what I've heard referred to as "man's reasoning on how to build a church." They believe the answer to their church's problems is more prayer. But if it were simply a matter of prayer we know MANY churches that should be having a HUGE impact on their communities. Unfortunately, they aren't. This is because there is both a spiritual and a natural side to pastoring.

This book deals with the natural side. It is intended to be extremely practical. *We won't spend much time on the spiritual aspects of ministry in a Post-Christian climate.* We are making the assumption that pastors already understand the importance of prayer and seeking God. Without the wisdom, power and blessing of God none of what we do makes a difference.[11]

Regardless of what we've written, church leaders have a responsibility to God and to the people they are called to serve to seek Him and get His perspective. If you just do what you read here because it's in a book you've failed in your primary mission: following Jesus, the Head of the Church. On the contrary, we know that many of the men and women who read this book will take these principles before God and ask Him how to apply them. And He will give them better ideas than ours on how to make this work!

Our prayer is that God would give you clarity concerning the next steps for your church. We pray that God would make you like the "Men of Issachar." In 1 Chronicles 12:32 we read that they "understood the times and knew what Israel should do." May He give you both the wisdom and understanding necessary to read the cultural tea leaves and implement a strategy that will impact many lives!

While this urgent message can seem foreboding, it is actually an **amazing opportunity** for the Church to take new ground for the Kingdom of God. He sees the future and isn't threatened by it. If we will listen to Him, He will help us make the necessary changes in order to meet this challenge head on. God has created us to be salt and light in the midst of a decaying, bland and very dark world.[12] Let's get on with it!

And let me add one final caveat. Because we read and listen to a lot of leadership material there are many thoughts and concepts that we've picked up from some amazing leaders and thinkers along the way. It's inevitable that we have included a quote or thought that isn't our own. If we have failed to quote a source it is purely unintentional.

- Jon & Robin Perrin

SECTION 1
America's Cultural Shift

Chapter 1
Our Story (In A Nutshell)

After finishing Bible school, we "officially" entered ministry in stereotypical non-denominational churches. We married a few years later and ended up as youth pastors at a Charismatic church in a low-income neighborhood. Although we loved and discipled our youth group students, we realized that in our church's neighborhood there were a LOT of unreached wannabe-gangster teens. *Challenge accepted!* We tried everything we could think of… we played basketball, went to school and sporting events, met with students at school lunches and ate way too much fast food with them.

We invested heavily in relationships with them. After almost five years of hard work, proving ourselves to be "normal" adults that loved students, we saw a dozens of these neighborhood students commit their lives to Christ in three weeks' time! I know that sounds like a small thing, but these were *our* kids! We had prayed for them, played with them and counseled them. We had *earned* the right to share Christ with them, and it had paid off richly!

From there our path took us to a healthy, fast-growing church in the north Dallas suburbs. Talk about culture shock! Up to that point we had worked with students that life had overlooked. Now we were working with very affluent students. As the pastor, Dr. Gerald Brooks, said: "God calls most pastors to comfort the afflicted, but here we have to afflict the comfortable." Once again, investing relationally in the day-to-day lives of students paid off richly.

It was at this church that I learned the nature of leadership. I call my years here a "Leadership Boot Camp." I was stretched beyond what I thought possible. It was truly the best of times and the worst of times. But it prepared us for what we would face in the future. And Pastor Brooks has been a pastor, a mentor and a spiritual father to me.

After seven years everything changed! We had accepted an invitation to teach in a German Bible school for a week. A few months before the trip, as we were praying for Germany and the people we would speak to, God interrupted my prayer time with an "inner voice" that was so loud it almost seemed as if I heard it audibly: "Don't just prepare to go to Germany for a week. Prepare to move your family there." WHAT?!?! It shook me to my core. Robin wasn't convinced, but within a few weeks God had revealed it to her as well.

Eight months later – three weeks after 9/11 – we landed in Frankfurt, Germany with our three small children, 17 suitcases, 3 car seats and hearts full of dreams! We joined an amazing team that worked to establish a church and Bible school in Bonn, Germany. We served in many different areas of church ministry, as well as teaching in the Bible school. Our major focus at that time was developing youth and worship leaders – especially those in small churches that couldn't afford to go to the big conferences. We also helped plant churches and youth groups across central Europe.

It took us a little while to get out of our Christian comfort zone. But in our quest to reach our neighbors for Christ, we were willing to do whatever necessary – even if it meant adjusting our normal style – to reach them. We were *desperate* for God to use us.

We quickly learned that the American Church subculture – everything from insider language, to Christian music and T-shirts, etc. – had absolutely NO connection to their world. It was as foreign to them as their culture was to us. So we did what all missionaries must learn to do if they want to be successful – we adapted!

We looked for opportunities to connect with our neighbors in any way we could. This included talking with them at every opportunity, inviting our neighbors over for dinner, inviting their kids to play with our kids, giving creative and fun Gospel presentations at our kids' birthday parties, performing in concerts at street festivals and bars... even hosting a neighborhood Easter Egg Hunt in our small village. Each of these gave us influence and opened further doors for us because we were not "preachy."

After 7 years in Bonn, we moved to southwestern Germany to focus on training, mentoring and coaching European church planters, pastors and church leaders. And since we were no longer serving on the pastoral staff of a church, we finally had the opportunity to experience churches from the *outside looking in*, rather than from the *inside looking out*. We visited nearly two dozen churches in our surrounding area in our quest for a church home for our family. We blogged about our experiences on our Perrin Ministries Leadership Blog under the title, "We are Visitors."[13]

While visiting these churches we noticed some areas that were, unfortunately, fairly consistent - areas which could definitely deter a visitor from returning:

- Boring, disorganized or toxic kids ministry
- Unfriendly church members that ignored visitors so they could "fellowship" with one another
- Using insider language (words or expressions that are only used within a church setting) – especially in the worship songs
- Facilities that were dirty or in poor condition – things which could have been fixed or cleaned relatively inexpensively
- The sound was distracting (too loud, too quiet, bad overall mix, etc.)
- The speakers or worship teams were unprepared

- Lifeless, dull sermons that were more theoretical than practical

Many of these churches worked very hard to attract visitors. We wondered why they would then shoot themselves in the foot by doing things to marginalize, embarrass or ostracize the very people they had prayed so passionately for and worked so hard to reach. Our conclusion was that if churches truly do want to reach the unreached they need to be willing to make some adjustments to their *situation normal.*

After a couple of years of this God again "spoke" to us… actually, this time it came to both Robin and I simultaneously. God was talking to me about taking crazy risks for Him, while at the same time He was talking with Robin about planting a church. After much prayer we felt we should plant a church in Freiburg, Germany.

We began to pray in earnest for what this church should be about and for a team of people to help us plant it. The more we prayed certain things became crystal clear. We were to plant "a church for those that don't do church." This made sense because less than 2% of the nearly quarter million residents of Freiburg are involved in a church.

Our four core values were to be:

- Authentic faith
- A safe place for people to investigate Christianity
- Family-friendly ministry with a focus on kids
- Outward-focused (serving with no strings attached)

Alongside these were some cultural values that were to define who we were to become and how we were to do things:

- Leadership development – Situational leadership was expected and celebrated. (We'll explain this later.)
- Risk-taking – Not being afraid to make mistakes. As leadership consultant Tony Morgan says, "The bigger risk is to never engage the unknown."

- Excellence – Doing the very best we can with what we have. Contrary to popular belief, excellence is not the same as perfection. While we give people grace to make mistakes, we choose to learn from these mistakes and continually get better.

- Problem-solving – To quote Matt Keller, pastor of Next Level Church in Fort Myers, Florida: "We're church planters. We don't take 'no' for an answer. We just get it done!"

- Taking ownership – This is MY church! I will do my part to make it better, and to help us to reach God's dream for our church.

- Presence – Be fully present! It's all about the journey. People are more valuable than programs. We can't afford to neglect the people around us just so we can reach our goals or fulfill our duties.

One important thing to note is that we realized kids in Germany were devalued. Of course their parents loved them, but they were often corrected and disciplined – even in churches – by harsh criticism and shaming. In our hearts we knew that we were to be a church that truly *celebrated* kids – not just *tolerated* them. And God brought alongside us an AMAZING team of people to help make that happen.

We will forever be grateful to the passionate, selfless visionaries that helped us plant our church. We would not have survived the launch phase of our church without them. They threw themselves into helping us build a thriving, life-giving church.

Of course we realize, "Unless the Lord builds the house, the builders labor in vain."[14] The reason our church experienced the rapid growth and results it did wasn't because we had the most talented or gifted team. God was truly at work. His fingerprints were all over it! But because our pastor taught us to pay attention and analyze everything we were able to identify some common denominators that led to our church's success. Thankfully these concepts are transferrable and will work for your church too!

Over the course of this book we will relate more stories concerning this church and what we learned through it. We just wanted to give you some cliff notes from our background so you will better understand our perspective as you read. Anytime this book refers to "Watermark" or "our church" it means this amazing church plant God allowed us to experience.

Chapter 2
The Winds Of Change

The USA is experiencing a radical cultural shift right now. It's INCREDIBLY different from the country that we left in 2001 when moving to Germany. We have been amazed at the changes. When we left, a church was a respected place. But there's an agenda (political, social, atheistic, demonic or otherwise) that is attempting to completely remove the influence of Christianity and the Church from North American society. And to be honest, it's been disturbingly successful.

It's not that the American church subculture is bad or wrong. But because of it believers have become so *insulated* and *isolated* from the world around them that they've lost their influence. The trend of young adults abandoning churches and forsaking their faith is well documented. A recent Barna Group survey points out that only three percent of non-Christian 20 - 30 year-old Americans hold a favorable view of evangelicals. David Kinnaman, president of Barna Group adds, "For non-Christian Millennials, the 'brand' of the Bible is a negative one."

[15] The American Church has become known by what it stands against rather than what it stands for. And while our culture is rapidly moving away from traditional Christian values the North American Church huddles in its safe little world.

A song many of us grew up singing in Kids Church was *This Little Light of Mine.* I think we've forgotten the context of Jesus' words, as recorded by Matthew. God created us to be lights to this dark world, to shine like a city on a hilltop.[16] Actually, the Bible informs us that light is to *shine in the darkness.*[17]

But in our quest to be separate from the world[18] we've become lights *shining among other lights.*

Societal Changes

In Europe we've seen the consequences that follow the removal of Christian influence from a society. The natural cultural progression passes from Modernism through Postmodernism and on to Secularism. Rather than rehashing what many great sociologists and scholars have already written, I will give a brief summary of each one to show the differences in societal changes.

- **Modernism:** Hedonism. The goal is getting all you can and then building a big fence around it.

    o Everything needs to be the biggest and the best in order to show a person's/organization's importance and value.

    o Churches strive to be relevant through professional quality, highly produced services. Big and flashy are extremely important.

    o The focus is on rational thought. Everything has to have a reason and make sense. In churches, apologetics are very useful. People are open to spiritual discussions, as long as they meet a felt need or are based on logical arguments.

- **Postmodernism:** A defining word is, "Whatever." Postmodernism maintains a cynical, disconnected worldview that questions everything.

    o Relativism reigns. This is epitomized by the phrase, "Your truth isn't necessarily my truth." To quote the Book of Judges: "...all the people did whatever seemed right in their own eyes."[19] Early in my ministry I was teaching a couple of young leaders when one of them pushed back against the concept of absolute truth. As the conversation progressed I was a bit shocked. He said that everyone is morally right because they do what works for them. I asked about

Hitler and his mission to eradicate the Jews. He replied that Hitler did what worked for him. I know this is an extreme example, but it personifies the mindset.

Another word to define this relativistic mindset is *deconstructionism*, which states that everything is relative to the hearer, reader or viewer of content. In other words, what I say means something to me. I convey thoughts from my worldview and experience. But my words may have a totally different meaning to the ones hearing what I say, due to their worldview and experiences. And the hearer's perception of what I say is just as valid as what I said and meant. Unfortunately, when applied to society it means that everything, including the Bible and faith in God, is relative.

o Tolerance – the belief that every viewpoint and truth claim is equally valid, as long as it doesn't assert its right to supersede another – is considered a virtue. And any idea or truth claim that professes to be superior (morally or otherwise) is labeled "intolerant," and therefore is actually LESS valid. It is, however, acceptable to not tolerate those deemed intolerant.

o A laissez faire attitude toward moral and spiritual issues is alive and well. Nihilism (everything is meaningless) is the result, thus the cynical attitude.

o In contrast to the flash and glitz of previous generations, authenticity is highly valued. At one point we pastored a group of neo-hippies that loved nothing more than to turn out the lights, illuminate the stage with candles and sing "touchy-feely" worship songs while someone painted at the side of the stage. I must admit, this was a lot of fun!

21

o People are still open to spiritual conversations as long as the Gospel is presented in an authentic manner. I once heard a pastor say of this generation, "Wow is out; real is in." In churches there needs to be a much greater emphasis on truth, but it needs to be presented in an *experiential* manner.

- **Secularism (Post-Christianity):** In a Post-Christian culture world religion has absolutely no influence on society. Churches and ministers are considered totally irrelevant to life in "the real world."

  o According to a 2013 survey by the Barna Group, 37% of US adults qualify as Post-Christian. 48% of Mosaics (adults aged 18 - 28) meet Barna's definition.[20]

  o Religion is considered a crutch for the weak, the ignorant or the hopelessly old-fashioned. The prevailing attitude toward church and Christianity eventually evolves from apathy to hostility.

  While I was in former East Germany helping my friend start a youth group I spoke with a group of teens. I began asking questions about their world. The conversation was great – they were as interested in my American world as I was in their German world – until I asked them to come to a party sponsored by the church. As soon as I mentioned "church" the critical questions and sarcasm started. Because I refused to be offended and responded patiently and respectfully quite a few of them attended our party – and three of them committed their lives to Christ!

  o As society grows more anti-Christian it will become increasingly more difficult for churches to find meeting locations, gain the necessary official permission for events and outreaches, maintain a positive "brand" and gain influence in the community. Many American communities now forbid renting public facilities (including school facilities) to religious organizations, especially to churches... and this trend is growing.

o As the influence of the Judeo-Christian moral values is removed, people become more selfish – only looking out for themselves. Things such as common courtesy and politeness will become more and more rare. Other than the occasional social gathering, many people will become more isolated than ever. The end result is cynicism.

o Social justice is an important value, whether that means feeding starving children, serving AIDS victims, fighting to end modern-day slavery or protecting the environment. The goal is to right the wrongs in the world, giving everyone a fair chance at a good life. Grassroots movements that tap into the social justice zeitgeist can gain traction quickly.

o Even within this setting spiritual conversations still happen as long as they occur within the context of authentic relationships. You will have to do a LOT of listening to earn the right to be heard. It's more effective to connect emotionally and relationally than have solid theological/logical arguments.

o People are spiritually open, but they are not interested in organized religion of any sort. If you can connect with them relationally you can sometimes bypass their defenses, as long as they don't feel like an "evangelistic project." The good news is that those who grow up without the influence of a church are not inoculated against Christianity.

Having lived in Europe for 13 years, we've seen the future of the American Church and it isn't pretty! Unless we make some drastic changes, we are in danger of becoming exactly like so many of the churches in Germany – irrelevant!

The State Of The American Church

Current statistics on the state of American churches are painfully staggering:

- 80% of all churches are in stagnation or decline.[21] About 4,000 churches close their doors every year in America, while only 1,000 new churches are planted.[22]

- **Young church dropouts**

    o 94% (some say 86%) of evangelical youth drop out of church after high school, *never to return*.[23]

    o According to Dr. Kara Powell, Executive Director of the Fuller Youth Institute, between 40 - 50% of students that are *actively* involved in church during their senior year of high school will drift away from the church after graduation. She encourages pastors to take a mental snapshot of all the young people in their churches. Then she tells them to ***draw a red X through half of them***.[24] If our churches don't change this will only get worse, and it is not acceptable!

    o The Barna Group has identified three subgroups within these "church dropouts"

        ▪ **Nomads:** They have walked away from church engagement but still consider themselves Christians.

        ▪ **Prodigals:** They have abandoned their faith altogether. Many claim that their Christian beliefs don't make sense to them.

- **Exiles:** They struggle to connect their faith or church with their everyday lives, and yet they continue in their Christian faith. Although they continue to attend a church (or churches), they find it increasingly difficult to live out their faith in a church setting.[25]

- **Rise of the "Nones"**
  - o The number of "Nones" – those that claim no religious affiliation – is the fastest growing religious group in American Culture.[26]
  - o 21% of Americans claim no formal religious identity, **more than doubling in number over the last two decades**.[27]
  - o 32% of adults under 30 have **no** religious affiliation.[28]

- Recent research by the Barna Group also revealed that even though the majority of Americans still consider themselves either Christian or "deeply spiritual," the gulf between their proclaimed beliefs and real actions is widening.[29]

We can't afford to simply stick our heads in the sand and ignore the problem. It's here to stay, and, unfortunately, the problem is growing steadily worse.

It's not that people hold animosity against the church. Some do. But most are simply indifferent, using statements like: "Leave me alone... you have nothing to offer me," or, "I'm not interested." They epitomize the quote from Homer Simpson flipping feverishly through the Bible in *The Simpsons Movie*: "This book doesn't have any answers!" As far as they are concerned, neither does the Church.

In Europe, the Church as a whole is dying. Muslims are buying Catholic Church buildings and turning them into mosques or Muslim cultural centers. Atheism and Satanism are on the rise. Berlin, Germany recently gave atheist students their own public holiday... June 21 – World Humanist Day. And almost no one listens to what believers or churches have to say.

As a matter of fact, as we prepared to launch our church we handed out invitations for our launch service along with a small piece of chocolate so people would accept the invitation. One man stopped me and asked, "Freiburg is full of empty churches. Why do we need another one?" It's tempting to get frustrated with such a question. Why even waste the time and energy responding? But I found it to be a fair question. If I can't answer the "why" question, I have no business planting – much less leading – a church.

I responded by explaining that the very reason why Freiburg needed another church was that many of the existing churches were empty. I suggested that perhaps what was needed was a different style of church, one that connected with "everyman," one that was geared towards people that have given up on church altogether.

Somewhere along the line we had stumbled upon a controversial, even radical idea, which we'll discuss in a bit. Of course we're not the first to notice it. Cultural "prophets" and forecasters have been talking about it for decades. And the marketing world certainly realizes it. It became the foundation for an amazingly evangelistic church that is still impacting the city of Freiburg, Germany.

Chapter 3
The Next Generations

The information in this book needs to be viewed against the mindset of the Millennials (a.k.a. Gen Y or Mosaics, the generation born from the early 1980s to the mid-2000s), iGen (a.k.a. Generation Z, Digital Natives, Generation@ or 2Ks – those born from the early 2000s to the present) and the generations that will follow. If we fail to understand today's kids, youth and young adults we will inevitably come to the wrong conclusions and make uninformed decisions.

Articles and resources concerning Millennials are widely available on the Internet, so I am not going to attempt an exhaustive treatise on the subject. But I do want to give you some cliff notes to help understand them. These are, of course, *sweeping generalizations* for a very *eclectic* and *individualistic* generation, but by and large they represent the people that will (hopefully) populate our churches over the next few decades.

Let me add that although Robin and I are Gen Xers by birth, we can relate to and, in many ways, identify with the mindset of Millennials, especially as it concerns churches. God has privileged us to connect with and minister to this generation for many years. This seems to be our *sweet spot* in ministry.

- This generation is almost 80 million in number, about 15% of whom are Christians.[30]

- Gen X parents, who were neglected "Latchkey kids", are raising them. Over half of Gen Xers grew up in broken homes; and 1/3 of them were abused in some way or another. These Gen X parents grew up robbed of the hope that should characterize childhood, and will do everything in their power to ensure their children experience a positive upbringing.

- This has produced what has been called *delayed adolescence*. It seems there are no rites of passage into adulthood anymore. Many of today's young adults still live with their parents into their late 20s and early 30s.

- They have a sense of entitlement, believing that they have the right to something – that they are due it, and it should be given to them NOW. They believe they don't need to do anything to earn it; they simply deserve it. They feel the world OWES them something.

  o Their hovering "helicopter parents" – ever-ready to swoop in and rescue them at the first sign of trouble – have empowered them to believe that the world will adjust to meet their needs. Their schools gave *everyone* a trophy at competitions or sporting events just for showing up. This has caused them to be egocentric, expecting to be catered to. And it may cause significant problems for their employers.

  o This generation no longer trusts authority figures. They have learned that anyone can find any answer by simply going online. When I was growing up you had to go through an expert to get answers. Now anyone can be an expert.

  o The vast array of choices available to them has produced a hyper-consumer mindset: "If you don't give me what I want, I'll just go somewhere else to get it."

  o In Jesus' *Prodigal Son* parable, the younger son illustrates this mindset perfectly. He says, "Father, GIVE ME what's mine!"[31] (What's crazy about this statement is that it didn't even belong to him yet!)

- Things such as money, prestige or position aren't as important to this generation as experience. They want to count their lives by the number of experiences they've had, not by the number of years they've worked. They want to live simply and authentically, but often don't know how to do so. And naturally they want their churches to reflect their values.

> o Nisha Gupta writes, *"But with all these opportunities at our fingertips, we become overwhelmed at the idea of having to choose just one. We become little kids in an ice cream shop; so many wonderful flavors, so hard to pick between them all! Infinite options lead to infinite indecision. So we think to ourselves, instead of selecting just one path, why not experience them all? And that's exactly what we end up doing.*
>
> *We are the slash/slash generation – a group of people that define ourselves not by a single occupation, but by the diversity of our experiences, passions and networks. Instead of carving out an upward trajectory life path within one career, we seek to gather as many experiences as possible to contribute to our multi-faceted lifestyle. It's more about creating a lifestyle than a life path. And the more multi-faceted the better."*[32]

- They are looking for a cause greater than themselves, something worthy of their time and investment, all the while hoping to discover who they are. This search for meaning is actually a defining characteristic of this generation. But because they are impatient with the process many never persevere long enough to discover their purpose. This causes older generations to consider them flighty or unreliable, but it is simply a result of the world in which they've been raised.

- They are often willing to commit to causes they connect with on an emotional level. Social justice is their rallying cry. They are a generation that doesn't just talk about making a difference; they are willing to act. And they are not afraid of doing the dirty work, as long as it accomplishes a significant purpose. They are not impressed with ostentatious displays of self-importance.

Because of this our ministries and outreaches need to be authentic, decentralized and focused on others rather than ourselves.

• They have only known a world with Internet, mobile phones, social media and texting, making them extremely tech savvy – and tech-dependent. And they prefer to get their news from Twitter feeds and late night comedians.

• Concerning work and finances, one in three prioritize freedom over salary.[33] Whereas the Baby Boomer generation lived to work and often remained with the same employer throughout their career, Millennials mostly work to live… just doing what is required to make enough money in order to live the life they want to live.

    o A recent Georgetown University study revealed that Millennials between ages 18 and 25 currently switch jobs 6.3 times during that time period.[34]

• Because they live in a multicultural, connected world, they consider themselves global citizens, sometimes feeling more of a global connection than a local one. This leads them to seek out overseas adventures. A friend in a large multinational company told us of a 20-something that worked for him. He first requested (and was given) an extended leave of absence so he could backpack through Europe. Then, when this young man made a similar request for another trip, his request was denied. So he simply quit in order to chase more backpacking adventures.

• They have taken relativism to the next level. They are open-minded and multi-cultural. While postmoderns value *tolerance*, Millennials emphasize *acceptance* and *support* for alternative viewpoints and lifestyles (with the important exception of those they deem *intolerant*). Many will assert their independence by "claiming" beliefs that are in opposition to those of their parents.

- Their pluralistic worldview makes it hard for them to connect the dots – tying what they do believe to corresponding action. They are comfortable living with contradictions, which frustrates older generations.

  For instance, in one of our Bible studies a young believer explained that he felt it was okay for him to lie if it kept him out of trouble. Another believer told us that her alcohol addiction didn't affect her credibility when sharing her faith, which she claimed to do "all the time." A young couple in our church told me it was okay for them to live together – even though they told me they knew the Bible instructs otherwise – because they were going to get married eventually. This mindset makes the discipleship process extremely messy!

- They value community (especially online connections) and are team-oriented, although their commitment to community looks very different than that of the preceding generations. Due to the highly mobile society in which live they understand that relationships are temporary. They tend to form deep friendships quickly, but are also able to let them go just as quickly. Whether or not this will lead to a higher divorce rate remains to be seen, if they marry at all. Many are choosing to live together and have children together, but never marry. The rise in the number of single mothers echoes this fact.

- Since so many of their connections are online they are more disconnected than ever from face-to-face interpersonal relationships, leaving them lonelier than ever. Combine this with Post-Christianity and you have a generation that will be progressively less involved and less interested in church, which they see as organized religion.

  o By and large they shun traditional denominations because these are seen as the "face" of organized religion. This mirrors the general shift in church attendance away from denominational churches.[35]

> o Many of the unchurched Millennials we know don't have a problem with Jesus. They just dislike His Church.

- According to Barna Group research concerning Millennials' view of the Bible, nearly half of non-Christian Millennials believe the Bible is just another book of teachings written by men that contains stories and advice. But the statistics actually get worse...

> o 30% of non-Christian Millennials relegate the Bible to merely a "useful book of moral teachings."

> o 19% say the Bible is "an outdated book with no relevance for today."

> o 27% go so far as to say the Bible is "a dangerous book of religious dogma used for centuries to oppress people."

> o When asked to identify words they associate with the Bible, non-Christian Millennials said: "story" (50%), "mythology" (38%), "symbolic" (36%), "fairy tale" (30%) and "historical" (30%).

> o 62% of non-Christian Millennials have never read the Bible.

> o On the other hand, for non-Christians whose Bible reading has increased in the past year (11%), the second most-cited reason for that increase is seeing how the Bible changed someone they knew for the better (27%). So, while seeing strangers reading the Bible in public may not be a positive catalyst, personal interactions with those who are affected for the better by the Bible are a strong recommendation for the Bible itself.[36]

- Concerning the Church:

o Rachel Held Evans does an excellent job of describing to pastors how Millennials view the Church: *"I explain how young adults perceive evangelical Christianity to be too political, too exclusive, old-fashioned, unconcerned with social justice and hostile to lesbian, gay, bisexual and transgender people. I point to research that shows young evangelicals often feel they have to choose between their intellectual integrity and their faith, between science and Christianity, between compassion and holiness. I talk about how the evangelical obsession with sex can make Christian living seem like little more than sticking to a list of rules, and how Millennials long for faith communities in which they are safe asking tough questions and wrestling with doubt."*[37]

o Young adults with Christian experience say the church is not a place that allows them to express doubts. They do not feel safe admitting that sometimes Christianity does not make sense. In addition, many feel that the church's response to doubt is trivial.[38]

o They wrestle with the exclusive nature of Christianity. Younger Americans have been shaped by a culture that esteems open-mindedness, tolerance and acceptance.[39] It is difficult for them to reconcile the two.

o Many feel church programs and "outreaches" are simply another marketing technique to get more people involved in the church (which is often true).

o In response too many pastors try to placate young adults by superficially tweaking the service style – things like music, stage design, media, lights and smoke, coffee bars, etc. But until the substance – the culture – of these churches changes, this generation won't be interested.

o Attendance patterns have radically changed. In the past we called a person a faithful attender if he or she was at our church *at least* three weekends out of the month. This generation considers themselves faithful attenders if they show up at church one or two times per month. In Germany we had people that told others Watermark was "their church," yet they only attended once every two to three months. If a person only gets judgment and guilt for their "lack of commitment" when he/she actually does come, you will probably see him/her less and less – if at all.

• But all hope is not lost. As bad as it seems, there are amazing opportunities to present God's grace this generation. We just have to adopt new ways of bringing the Gospel *into their world* instead of waiting for them to venture into our world. In other words, we have to start thinking out of the box if we want to reach them.

• We need to capitalize on the fact that they want to make an impact. They need to know that God created them with this innate desire. He designed them to live for a cause greater than them, and to change the world.

• Because their learning style is non-linear (rather than going from point A to point B, they may progress from point A to point D to point F to point C… not getting to point B for years), leaders, mentors and coaches need to be prepared to exhibit extreme patience and grace.

• Those willing to invest in (read: earn) a relationship with youth and young adults will find open hearts and open minds. Practical biblical teaching on relationships, grace, forgiveness, finances, purpose and hope can create opportunities to invite them to experience a life-giving church.

I understand that to some pastors these may seem like negative attributes. This doesn't mean that younger generations are flawed. These are simply the facts on the ground. They are neither good nor bad. It simply is what it is. We've got our work cut out for us!

We can lament and complain all we want, but it won't change anything. We will just have to learn how to engage this culture in a different way than we've done in the past. Actually, like all changes, we can view them as a problem or an opportunity. If we can learn how to adapt to any culture, we will thrive when others struggle, and we will still be flourishing in the future when the culture changes yet again.

Chapter 4
A Radical Approach

In the beginning Adam and Eve walked with God. They had an intimate relationship with Him. They intentionally chose something (*someone*) else rather than Him. And because God is holy (pure, perfect), their betrayal severed their relationship with Him. It separated them from Him. I believe He removed them from the Garden of Eden so they wouldn't be able to eat from one of the other trees in the garden: the Tree of Life. He didn't want them to live forever in that broken state.

But God wasn't finished yet. He came up with an amazing rescue plan. His plan to restore that relationship was unprecedented: He did it in person!

> *"Jesus took on flesh and blood and moved into the neighborhood."*
>
> *John 1:14 MSG*

Jesus came down to where we are. He actually *became* one of us. Not only was it the way to pay the penalty for our rebellion against God; it was an incredibly creative way to introduce God to us and us to God. The way He chose to connect with us was intensely personal. It wasn't through a theological textbook, but rather organic, earthy and raw. Jesus walked this earth, tasted the dust on the wind and smelled the fresh rain on the fields as He walked from village to village. The God of the universe had dirty feet. He experienced life just as we do. This was how He *chose* to engage with us.

But somewhere along the line the Church decided it was better to serve God in isolation. Our churches became monasteries. Outsiders were welcome to *visit*, but they never really *belonged*. Only after jumping through a lot of hoops (so that they looked, smelled and acted like us) did they qualify for membership in our spiritual club.

This may be the Western influence on Christianity. Our culture is one of fierce independence. But it wasn't like this with the Early Church...

As a matter of fact, among Jesus' last recorded words were,

> *"Go into the world. Go everywhere and announce the Message of God's good news to one and all."*

> *Mark 16:15 MSG*

Believers were expected to share what they had experienced with outsiders. This was God's plan all along. Through the ancient Jewish prophets God said He wanted to use Israel and its prosperity to capture the attention of a world that didn't even know He existed.[40]

The Apostle Paul understood something in the First Century that many of today's churches have forgotten. He knew the tension between trying to work within the prevailing culture while still holding fast to godly values and sound doctrine. He came to the conclusion that we can't absolve ourselves of the responsibility to engage this world just like Jesus did. He once wrote:

> *"I became all things to all people so that I might win some..."*

> *1 Corinthians 9:22*

He chose to engage the world head on, entering it as a missionary. It was risky, and it cost him dearly in some places. But it paid off richly! Because of Paul and others like him the Good News spread throughout the entire world.

A Safe Religion?

I know this is risky, but Christianity was never meant to be a safe religion. It cost Jesus and all but one of his disciples their very lives to establish the Church. We deceive ourselves when we think we can follow Jesus closely and live a safe life. It is

VERY DANGEROUS to follow Jesus. It will cost you everything, just as it did Him.

Our problem is that in Western society we are accustomed to comfort, security and safety. We make choices based on convenience rather than risk. I'll share my faith if it's convenient. I'll give to the poor if feel guilty enough. I'll serve my neighbor if he's being nice this week. I'll invest in a relationship if it's expedient (if I get something out of it). I'll attend church if I can squeeze it in or if I'm not too tired.

But God calls us to a life of faith. And faith is all about risk, the very enemy of convenience. He calls us to give of our time, our talents and our finances/stuff, even if there is no obvious payoff. He tells us to forgive those that have wronged us or taken advantage of us. He instructs us to do what's right, even if no one is looking.[41] He even commands us to take the message of His grace to the ends of the earth – which includes taking it next door.[42]

If we want to follow God's plan for our lives we will have to get out of our comfort zone, which is actually more like a prison. Pastors are skilled at challenging *others* to get out of *their* comfort zones while remaining safe within *their own*. But if we're going to lead our people into the green pastures that God has prepared for our churches there will be times when we have to walk through the valley of the shadow of death.[43] This is risky!

The Caesars pacified their people with free bread and the circuses (games and gladiatorial contests, which included having Christians and criminals fight lions and other beasts). Because the people were satisfied they didn't notice or care that the empire was descending into chaos, corruption was rife and Rome's enemies were invading.

I believe many "satisfied" people will barely make it into heaven (figuratively speaking), having nothing of eternal value to show for their life on earth. We'll see what could have been, and what should have been. We'll see all the missed and wasted opportunities. I believe this is why God will have to "wipe away all the tears from our eyes."[44]

I want to be able to present to God a life that was fully devoted to Him, obeying Him at all times, no matter what the cost. That is a legacy I want to leave to my children and those God has called me to lead. I'm not there yet, but this is my goal!

As our culture progressively becomes more secular this concept of convenience and safety will draw a line in the sand for us. Will we engage a world that promotes wrong as right? Will we take a stand for Jesus (and for morality) when it's not convenient? Will we serve God openly even though it becomes increasingly unpopular? Will we share the Good News in a hostile environment?

The secret that we learn from the Early Church in the Book of Acts is to have a regular rhythm of gathering and scattering. The believers gathered for encouragement and empowerment and then scattered for impact. This is the rhythm our churches will need to embrace if we are going to make a difference in a secular, Post-Christian society. Otherwise we will end up hiding inside our churches as if they were bomb shelters… and our churches will die.

The American Church must adopt this mindset in order to reach an increasingly unchurched society. The goal is to contextualize the Gospel so an unchurched world can connect with it. Unfortunately, Post-Christianity is not just headed this way, it's about to crash upon us like a tsunami. It promises to totally alter the landscape. But there is still time to adjust and prepare for it. And those that are prepared will find amazing opportunities in the midst of the spiritual chaos. It's not enough to be able to read the signs. We have to also understand the path forward.

Chapter 5
What To Expect

In *SECTION 2* we'll get into some nuts and bolts practical content. Over the years we've identified six areas that are *critical* to ministry in a Post-Christian context, especially among Millennials. You'll probably notice that all six flow in and out of each other. This is because they are interdependent, and are all vital to engaging the unchurched and de-churched in a secular world.

It is important to note that we are not endorsing a particular church model. I have described the vision, core values and strategy that God gave us, but ours is not the only valid church model. These six areas will help *any* church in *any* setting take steps in the right direction. Of course there are other factors that determine church health, but we've found these to be the most essential.

Each of these ingredients is like a building block. The more blocks, the broader your base can be. And the broader your base, the higher you can build. A number of churches already have one or more of these blocks integrated into their culture, which affects the impact they have on their communities. We've learned that the more of these blocks a church has in place, the more effective it will be with the next generations as our society moves farther from God.

The six critical components of effective ministry in a Post-Christian context are:

Authenticity – *Be Real.*

Aim – *Who You Are Determines Where You're Headed.*

Accessibility – *Welcoming The World With Open Arms.*

Alignment – *Empowering The People God Sends You.*

Action – *Getting Your Hands Dirty.*

Availability – *Family Matters.*

In *Section 3* we'll give some practical advice on how to implement what we've written. Often when reading a book like this we're tempted to try to change everything at once. Or to do the opposite – allow ourselves to be overwhelmed by all the changes we need to make. This section will help you take manageable steps that won't overwhelm your people. We have included thoughts for both senior leaders and for those in subordinate positions.

Finally, and most importantly, you need to understand that the principles in this book will be useless if we only seek to grow our churches. ***This is NOT a church growth manual!*** This is a book about engaging a culture that is sprinting away from God. We are called to BE the Church, not DO churchy things. We have to remember that unchurched people are not objects to be won, but rather people to be loved. Jesus called us to take the Gospel message to the lost and hurting, the desperate and the dying – this includes those that don't even know they need His help. Church growth will be a natural byproduct of becoming more like Christ in reaching out to the world.

Discussion Questions:

What challenges will Post-Christianity bring to churches?

How can a sense of entitlement hinder spiritual growth?

How can we motivate young leaders that aren't driven by money, position or power?

How do relativism and the Gospel clash? Can the two be reconciled? If so, how?

What unique opportunities do the intersection of Post-Christianity and the Millennial generation present for the Church?

SECTION 2
Six Components Of Effective
Post-Christian Ministry

AUTHENTICITY

Be Real

Because authenticity is such an integral part of Post-Christian culture – especially among Millennials – it is mentioned in nearly every chapter of this book. I do, however, need to establish a few important thoughts about being real. I *can't possibly overstate* its importance in our churches. Your church may be solid in every other area, but if you fail the authenticity test your ministry will be severely limited.

Chapter 6
Just Be Real

When we were associate pastors in Texas, a professional football superstar in our area asked if he could have a large Bible study in our church auditorium. Our pastor agreed, but only on the condition that he would first get my approval, since my young adults group met at the church on the same night.

To introduce us to each other my pastor invited both of us to lunch. This man was very personable and seemed very interested in what was happening in our church and what we were doing with the young adults. He asked a lot of questions about my family and me. I'm not going to lie to you... it was pretty awesome to have lunch with a future NFL Hall of Famer!

I, of course, gave him my blessing. His Bible study would have no impact on my group anyway. Our group members enjoyed football; but they loved each other and our vision even more. We decided to cancel our group meeting and come to his first Bible study to support what he was doing.

As usual I arrived early to make sure everything was setup and running smoothly. He also arrived early, just as the first of his group was starting to come in. I went to him to reintroduce myself and say hi. He recognized me and we chatted for a few seconds. My wife walked up and as I was introducing her some other people came into the building. He shook her hand and said hi as he looked over our heads to see who was coming in. It was as if he had given us "the wink and the gun," or the "What's up?" nod. Totally fake! He had been interested in me only because he needed my approval to do his thing. He had used us as a means to an end.

Just Another Customer

How many times have we been treated like this at a church? Not when you're the pastor, of course. Everyone wants the pastor's attention. But for a church visitor this is a typical experience.

I have to admit I'm sometimes guilty of this as well. My ADD kicks in and my mind drifts away from the conversation I'm having. I notice other people walking by and smile, nod or say hi as I continue my current conversation. I find it happens most often when I'm tired. Thankfully in our Freiburg church there was a young man that would call me on it when I started to check out. He would say, "I know you're busy and have a lot of people to talk to, but can I speak to you for a few minutes?" It brought me right back to our cultural value of being present.

On any given Sunday morning in North America a church visitor will encounter everything from fake smiles and handshakes to artificial passion and emotion. It's worse acting than what you find in a soap opera! Most people that have grown up in church are used to this. But unchurched people HATE it!

They are fed up with inauthenticity, and are quite sensitive to it. They are begging us to show them the real Jesus! But we can't do this if we're pretending to be something we're not. *No one* has this holiness thing figured out. No one's life is perfect; so why do we pretend ours is, as if we are somehow holier than someone else? Jesus warned us against this type of judgmental attitude.[45]

Let's instead open up and make ourselves vulnerable. *This* is the Christianity I read about in the Bible. And *this* is the brand of Christianity that will draw a cynical world to Christ.

Early into our time in Europe I was privileged to fly first class on an 11-hour flight from Frankfurt to Dallas. I was traveling a lot at the time and had accrued quite a few airline miles, which afforded me a complimentary upgrade. Flying international first class is SWEET! You start off with a warm moist towel for your face, warm roasted mixed nuts and juice or champagne. You enjoy hors d'oeuvres and steak or fish and fresh vegetables for your meal while everyone in the main cabin eats packaged pasta or chicken. For dessert you are treated to a custom-made sundae or bowl of fruit. And the cheese and wine cart passes by every hour or so. The personal movie player and power ports for your electronic devices are a huge plus. Needless to say, I was having a great day!

The stewardess for our section was quite friendly and had a fun attitude. Most of the other people in first class were asleep so she struck up a conversation with me as she came through the cabin. We talked for a long time. We talked about our families and what we enjoyed about our careers. We laughed about some of the strange passengers you encounter on airplanes and funny turbulence stories. She even told me of her plans for retirement.

After we landed I was waiting for my luggage in the baggage claim area. I saw this stewardess walking by and said, "Goodbye. Have a great day." She gave me a polite smile and kept walking. WOW! That entire conversation on the plane was simply her doing her job. I was *just another customer*. I wasn't expecting her to stop everything and hug me goodbye, but that truly caught me off guard. I get it... she was probably tired from a long day's work and just wanted to go home. But I felt devalued and duped.

How often do visitors experience this in even our most "friendly" churches? They arrive to a warm welcome; but after the service is over everyone goes about their business or hangs out with their friends, leaving the visitors feeling abandoned and duped. We can't afford to treat the precious visitors who come as God's answer to our prayers like this. If we truly value them, we will do everything we can to help them feel truly at home. When we have special guests in our home, we focus on getting everything ready for them so their stay is an especially pleasant one. We need to do this for our church guests as well.

Stand And Greet Time

Thom Rainer wrote a blog post that blew up across the Christian social media spectrum. On Twitter he asked first time church visitors what in a church service made them decide not to return. The number one response *by far* was the "Stand and greet time."[46] This is the, "Turn and give your neighbor a high five and tell them you're glad they're here" transition between the music/announcements and the preaching.

When he asked why, he received a wide range of responses, most of them very negative. There were comments such as "awkward" and "uncomfortable." One person commented, "In most of the churches it should be called a stand and fake it time. The members weren't friendly at all except for ninety seconds." Another replied, "I would rather have a root canal than be subjected to a stand and greet time."[47]

I'm not necessarily suggesting that you should get rid of the stand and greet time. I'm only asking you to evaluate what your church service looks like through the eyes of a visitor and adjust it to be more authentic, inviting and welcoming. If you are going to have a stand and greet time, at least explain *why* you're doing it.

We can't afford to do business as usual in a Post-Christian climate. Unchurched people have much better things to do than sit with a bunch of fake people for a couple of hours on their only day off. If they sense we're faking it they won't darken the doors of our churches. And I can't say I blame them.

Fake Churches

One of the big problems Robin and I have with the US church subculture is that, by and large, American churches are incredibly inauthentic (read: FAKE). The focus is on presenting the perfect stage show, and for everyone onstage to have a powerful *bigger than life* stage presence. What's valued is the ability to work the crowd, where every person on stage basically becomes a "front man." This, of course, lends itself to a lack of sincerity. It is important to note, however, that if your up-front people have no energy or personality, it will be more difficult to connect with a younger audience.

A big problem is that many of us are so insecure that we see pastoring and worship leading as an opportunity to showcase our gifts and talents. It satisfies our need for approval, to be on the big stage. So we approach it as a gig. It's a chance for us to do our thing… to play for the crowd. In the movie *Gladiator* we find Proximo, the aging former gladiator, giving some advice to Maximus, his star trainee: "Win the crowd." In other words, do whatever it takes to keep them coming back – entertain them, jump through the hoops, etc.

The natural result of this ideology is the belief that ministry is simply what happens on the stage, that everything else in the church is peripheral. Because it's all about the show people tend to devalue biblical community and the discipleship process. People may get spiritually *fed*, but they never get any spiritual *exercise* because the prevailing mindset is that only the professionals – church leaders – are responsible for results.

If we want to truly represent Jesus we *must* be authentic. He didn't fake anything. He was truly angry with the hypocritical religious leaders. His heart really did go out to the diseased, the broken and the outcasts. His compassion led Him to cry real tears when he saw his friends, Martha and Mary grieving over the death of their brother, Lazarus. As a matter of fact, The Apostle John, in his eyewitness account, records Jesus as being overcome with emotion three separate times during this one event.[48]

We can't afford to underestimate the crucial importance of being authentic. In a Post-Christian culture people are quick to spot someone who's fake, especially when he/she is a "religious" person. They've been marketed to all of their lives. They realize that everyone has an angle. As far as they are concerned, everyone wants to sell them something or get something from them.

The unchurched are crying out for us to be real. They are used to "Reality TV," which has very little to do with actual reality. They are quite familiar with media personalities and all their craziness. Although they do appreciate the entertainment value of all of this, they realize there is much more to life than all this absurdity and drama.

We must be real! We are all in the same boat. None of us has it all together. All of us are "damaged goods" that have been rescued and restored by Jesus Christ. Not one of us has this life all figured out. Anyone who says differently is either deceived or deceiving others. Why, then, would we stand up in front of people and act like we do? We need to share stories of failure as well as success. Everyone can relate to failure. It's the common denominator of human existence.[49]

Bait And Switch

One of the things that churches have become famous for is the old fashioned "bait and switch." It's a marketing ploy where a business lures someone into their store by offering an incredible deal on something the person really wants. But when the person arrives that item is "unfortunately" sold out. The store does, however, offer its customers something that is "actually a better product," but it comes with a higher price tag. You took the bait (the incredible deal) to come into their store, but they switched it with the product they actually wanted you to buy in the first place.

Let's examine how the bait and switch event plays out in a typical church scenario. A church member invites their cynical friend to a church event. This friend comes with the church member, meets a few people, has some fun... and then he/she is preached to. He/she came expecting to have fun, but instead got suckered into a pseudo church service (complete with all the weird traditions that churches are famous for).

They've been tricked! Now how much credibility do you think the church member will have the next time they try to invite this person (or anyone this person talks to about their experience) to a church event? More than likely, none.

We have to rethink our strategy! The bait and switch may have worked a couple of generations ago, but it's not very effective anymore. People today - especially Millennials - have too many other options. What if we, instead, offered a party where the entire goal was to get outsiders to hang out with our church people? What if we offered an event where people just came together for a meal to enjoy each other's company? We should at least teach our people to share what to expect when inviting someone to one of our events. And we should also train our people not to proselytize the visitors. Jesus will probably come up in a conversation naturally. We are, after all, Christ-followers. But we don't need to force it.

In the Gospel accounts of Jesus' life (Matthew, Mark, Luke & John) I've noticed that He NEVER offered a bait and switch. When you came to Him, you could always expect to receive "grace and truth." (John 1:14) The only ones to face His wrath and rebuke were those that believed they were somehow better than others, and that they were capable of pleasing God entirely on their own merits.

We have to get back to representing the true heart of Jesus. One of the church planters I mentor asked his people to invite their friends to "a church service with a baseball game afterwards." After the short service they grilled hotdogs, then headed over to a pro baseball game to have some fun together. No one was under any illusion as to what it was all about. It was a chance for people to visit the church and then watch a ballgame together afterward. And they DID have a number of happy visitors because this church was up front about what to expect.

Let's rethink how we do ministry. American culture is FULL of marketing ploys. As a result, people have become cynical and choosy about with whom they do business. Let's be truly authentic and actually EXCEED peoples' expectations! If we do, word of mouth will be our best friend.

Chapter 7
The Power Of Vulnerability

I was asked to be the keynote speaker in a weeklong youth outreach for unchurched international school students. We worked during the day building houses for Romanian gypsies and had "Club Meetings" (services) at night. I felt handicapped by the parameters they gave me: "Since this is an unchurched crowd you have to stay away from only teaching a Bible lesson or being overly 'Jesus-focused.'" They asked me to wait until the last night to talk about the Cross and the resurrection. On that last night I didn't even need my notes. I didn't have to focus on my delivery. Sharing the Gospel message with outsiders is so hard-wired into who I am that it just flowed out naturally. And they commented on how much better my talk was that night than on the other nights.

While I understand what they were trying to accomplish, I felt I wasn't allowed to be who I truly am. We are always the most effective when we are leading, speaking or serving from the center of who we authentically are. We need to speak from our hearts by teaching what we've learned or are learning. When we do this authentically, adding our own personal stories, we personify what was said about Jesus: "They had never heard teaching like this. It was apparent that he was living everything he was saying—quite a contrast to their religion teachers!"[50]

Even though Paul acted as a sort of chameleon, adjusting his style to connect with the culture of his audience, He knew exactly who he was and what he was called to do. It was never about pleasing people. Although he did adjust his delivery based on the setting, he never adjusted his content. His mission was to preach the Good News to a world that was far from

God. And he allowed no amount of trouble or persecution to stop him.

This adaptation to fit the context is much more than a pastor simply taking off his coat and tie, wearing skinny jeans or untucking his shirt. It is a *radical* cultural shift. It's not easy. You will pay a price for this (with your comfortable "church regulars"). But what is the alternative?

There is a fine line between adjusting to connect with the people to whom God is sending us and simply pretending to be like them. I'll never be a long-haired, pierced and tattooed, tie-dye and sandal-wearing pastor, even though I think that some people can pull it off amazingly. I have to be who I am – the father of three teenagers with a few more gray hairs than I care to admit. But I do need to develop an appreciation for those that are different than me, *even if* they wear skinny jeans.

One of the best ways pastors can connect with people groups that are radically different than them is to hire staff members that represent the diversity they want to see. It's important that they ask God to send them someone that can connect with the demographic they believe He's calling them to reach. If you want to reach more young adults, consider recruiting younger leaders/staff that will connect with this crowd. If you wish to reach more young families (and *you* don't have young children), ask God to send you someone that can connect with this precious group.

Even though our children were pre-teens/early teens when we started our church, God was very clear that our target audience was to be twenty- and thirty-somethings. We targeted our Facebook advertising, our website, posters, flyers and all our marketing tools toward this demographic in the Freiburg, Germany area. We knew that we couldn't market to people our age if we wanted to reach the people God to whom God had sent us.

We wanted to gain brand recognition with our logo and create the connection in people's minds between this logo and a different kind of church. So we found some young guys with fresh ideas to create our web and print graphics, even though

Robin holds a degree in Marketing. Since we didn't have many connections in Freiburg we used social media almost exclusively to launch our church.

Our marketing also reflected our desire to be branded as the "Rock-n-roll Coffee Church" in Freiburg, which both represented who we were as a church and the demographic we knew we were called to reach – the young, hipster German / international crowd. Fortunately for us the "cool church" style was cutting edge ministry in Germany. We were able to create a life-giving American style church and it really connected with the young adults we were called to reach in Freiburg.

One thing that helped was that every piece of our advertising or marketing showed that children were *valued* at our church, not just *tolerated*. And because German and immigrant parents wanted their kids to learn English our bilingual Kids Church was wildly popular in our area. In the end, we prayed A LOT for God to send us people with the same passion for this generation to help us plant this church. He did!

The Church "Game Face"

Growing up in a Charismatic/Word of Faith church, I learned as a young teenager that your words carry power.[51] Because of this we were taught to watch our words and be careful to make a "good confession."[52] Don't get me wrong, I believe this is a solid biblical principle. But somehow many from my spiritual background never learn to balance this principle with the principle of authenticity. As a result, there are a number of churches that never experience the true Christian community God desires our churches to have. I cover this topic in more detail in the chapters on Availability.

One thing I love about the Bible is that God made sure the good, the bad and the very ugly parts of the lives of a number of biblical characters were recorded. We read about their triumphs as well as their failures. The Apostle Paul wrote that these things were to serve as examples to teach us.[53] These stories help us process what it means to pursue God in the real world – the struggles we will face, the emotions we will have to overcome and the payoff for our perseverance.

Unfortunately, in many churches people are so concerned with putting on their church "game face" – a *mask* to hide their brokenness – that they never open up and find healing. It's pointless to go to a doctor but not share all your troubling symptoms with her. She can't make a correct diagnosis and put you on the path to health without all the information. I heard one doctor say that there are just as many sick people walking the streets as there are in hospitals (probably more!). It's the ones in the hospital that are getting help. But in order to receive that help we've got to admit that we're broken and in need.

Several biblical "faith giants" – even Jesus Himself – reveal the vital importance of letting our guard down with our circle of friends so they comfort and encourage us, and strengthen our resolve.

- David – When King Saul tried to kill him, he went to his best friend, the king's son, Jonathan, to process why the king would act in such a way and what he could do about it.[54]

- Peter and John — When they were threatened by the religious authorities for performing a miracle and preaching about Jesus, they went back to a group of their fellow believers, who encouraged them and prayed for them.[55]

- Paul – He shared with his church plant in Corinth the struggles he had experienced while ministering in the province of Asia: "We were under great pressure, far beyond our ability to endure, so that we despaired of life itself."[56]

- Jesus – He invited his closest followers into His intense emotional struggle and a time of prayer as He saw the crucifixion approaching: "My soul is overwhelmed with sorrow to the point of death. Stay here and keep watch with me."[57]

In each of these instances we see the choice to lean into community and relationships, not run from them.

Vulnerability

Authenticity and vulnerability go hand in hand. In order for our people to feel that we are worthy of their trust we have to make ourselves vulnerable. That means opening up about our struggles, fears and failures. It means admitting that we're a work in progress when it comes to the principles we are teaching. It means acknowledging that we don't always get it right when we try to hear from and obey God. It means that if we don't have the answer we don't pretend as if we do. It's absolutely okay to say, "I don't know…" or "I'm not sure, but I'll look into it and get back with you."

On the other hand, we can't fall apart when something goes wrong. Our people will lose confidence in us if we can't handle the pressures of leading. Leaders have to be strong and confident in who God has called them to be and what He has called them to do. Vulnerability simply means we don't hide our weakness (our humanity). Some of the pastors I most respect is those that admit they are seeing counselors regularly. To me this doesn't mean they are weak. It means they are honest. And it gives me hope.

Our natural pushback to this concept is that we feel people won't respect us if they realize we aren't perfect… or at least that we aren't who they thought we were. This may be true of some shallow people. But I'm going to let you in on a little secret – most people already realize that we have flaws. And those that don't will eventually figure it out.

I need to add that there are some struggles we don't need to make public until they are conquered. Perry Noble has done an excellent job of talking about his struggles with debt, pornography and depression. But he has spoken of each of these *after* he has come through the other side of "the valley of the shadow of death."[58]

Safe Places

In order for vulnerability to take place in a church it must first become a safe place. It is this safety that creates the atmosphere where vulnerability can thrive. If people feel they will be judged for sharing their weaknesses, emotions, failures and struggles they will never open up.

This MUST come from the top down! When pastors choose to make themselves vulnerable they set the tone for the congregation. They show their people that it is okay to struggle with doubts, fears, anger, frustration, hurt and disappointment. This is exactly what Jesus instructed His disciples to do. He told them, "Keep open house; be generous with your lives. By opening up to others, you'll prompt people to open up with God, this generous Father in heaven."[59]

It is through the intentional creation of this type of environment that visitors feel truly welcome. They aren't simply customers, but rather welcomed guests. It is also a way to encourage people to connect in small groups. If your small groups promise more of what people have come to enjoy about your church you will have a much better chance of attracting them to get involved.

Creating An Authentic Culture

Authenticity is the most important of the six components we discovered. It provides the atmosphere for the other five components to function correctly. It is also the hardest of them to build into a church culture. It doesn't happen by accident. We'll discuss how to change the culture of your organization in the chapters on Aim. But let me give you a few pointers that apply specifically to authenticity.

As I've said, creating a culture of authenticity has to come from the top down. In other words, the pastor and leadership of the church have to model the vulnerability they want their congregation to embrace. Culture is caught, not taught. Creating this environment doesn't happen simply through teaching, sharp promo materials, a church-wide campaign or a vision statement. It only happens when the leaders – beginning with the Senior/Lead Pastor and his/her Executive Team – choose to make themselves vulnerable by opening up their lives to the people around them.

Creating this culture of authenticity is partially accomplished in the weekend services – during the announcements, worship, sermon, ministry time, etc. But what is most effective is when it shows up in the genuine friendships among the leadership/staff. Having regular team playtimes, meals and offsite meetings/retreats can help create this atmosphere. The team that plays and prays together typically stays together. Shared experiences – both fun and challenging – go a long way in creating open and honest dialog between colleagues. Let's be honest... in the office we're usually all about one thing: the bottom line. Having group activities (where we don't focus on church issues) allows us to "let our hair down."

If we want our church members to buy into the small group concept, we've got to buy in ourselves – we've got to *live* it. What better way than making each area of ministry its own small group? The pastoral staff can be a small group, just as the youth ministry, Kids Church and usher teams can. We'll discuss small groups further in the chapters on Availability, but know that this is a powerful way to develop the authentic relationships God wants us to have.

We have included some diagnostic questions for this and the rest of the core components on the http://PostChristianTsunami.com website.

Discussion Questions:

Why is authenticity so important to the unchurched, especially Millennials?

Why do you think authenticity is so rare in churches?

Have there been areas in your life where you've been faking it? What about in your church services?

How can you encourage your church members and leaders to be more authentic?

What practical steps can you take to make your church a safe place?

AIM

Who You Are Determines Where You're Headed

This refers to your church's DNA. What has God called your church to be? Churches aren't called to be carbon copies of one another. They are to be as unique as the individuals that call them home. If a church's leaders can determine what God has called their church to be, they will be able to determine their target audience and an effective strategy.

Chapter 8
Your Church's DNA

King David stood up and said, "Listen to me, my relatives and my people. I wanted to build a place to keep the Ark of the Agreement with the Lord. I wanted it to be God's footstool. So I made plans to build a temple. But God said to me, 'You must not build a temple for worshiping me, because you are a soldier and have killed many people.'

The Lord said to me, 'Your son Solomon will build my Temple and its courtyards. I have chosen Solomon to be my son, and I will be his father. He is obeying my laws and commands now. If he continues to obey them, I will make his kingdom strong forever.'"

[David said to his son,] "Solomon, you must understand this. The Lord has chosen you to build the Temple as his holy place. Be strong and finish the job."

David said, **"All these plans were written with the Lord guiding me. He helped me understand everything in the plans."** *[emphasis mine]*

1 Chronicles 28:2-3, 6-7, 10, 19 NCV

King David lets us in on a secret to building a healthy, growing church (or organization): He got the plan directly from God. When it comes to our churches, we are called to be builders, not architects. The plans for each one have already been drawn up. We have to get with God and hear from Him in order to discover *His* plan for the church we've been called to lead.

61

God's Thumbprint

Each one of us is a unique creation. We have unique DNA, retinal patterns and fingerprints. Scientists even claim that each of us has a unique heartbeat. There is not one other person exactly like us among the 7 billion inhabitants of planet earth, nor has there ever been. Not even our twin is an exact replica. God made us this way. We are each called to represent a distinct aspect of the nature of God. He wants to reveal His heart and creativity to the world through each of our lives.

When God brings a group of these unique individuals together to form a local church, it stands to reason that they will be different from any other group of believers. God has a unique thumbprint (vision, mission, core values, culture) for each church. Our church wasn't created to look like the one down the street. Nor are we supposed to do things the same way the large church across town does them.

Too many churches are getting "cosmetic surgery" in order to look like another, more successful church. I heard a pastor once say that if you go into any church you can usually determine the last conference the pastoral staff attended. You can see it in their style of music, the words they use, the look of the stage and their preaching style. But we can't fulfill God's unique call for our body of believers while trying to be like another church.

In today's consumer culture some churches that experience "success" (usually defined as financial stability and numerical growth) package their program and monetize (sell) it. But when pastors of smaller churches purchase and try to implement this program they rarely get the same results. Why? It was God's thumbprint for a different church consisting of different people in a different setting. And often smaller churches copy the easy external things the church does rather than the best practices that made the bigger church successful in the first place.

There are, of course, principles that will work in any church setting, such as the ones we are laying out in this book. Principles are *always* transferrable. The application may be different, but biblical principles such as hospitality, grace, ministering to the hurting and celebrating kids will work in any church. Churches that have figured out how to apply these principles to their unique setting usually experience growth while many of the rest are in decline or have plateaued.

Thankfully there are some great organizations out there that help churches of all sizes discover their unique God-given DNA and how they are supposed to bring glory to God. But even with one of these organizations assisting us we cannot delegate our responsibility to seek God and discover His thumbprint for our church. The heartbeat of God is ascertained only by spending intimate time with Him.

Changing The Culture

In one of the churches we served we were asked to take over the small group program. Because most of the small group leaders were either Bible school students or graduates these groups had become either "worship fests" (Charismatics will understand this phrase) or long-winded teaching sessions. And attendance was dwindling.

Because the strength of this ministry – and especially that of the pastor – was teaching, most of the small group leaders did what they had seen and experienced in the church or the Bible school. And they focused on making sure their group members' doctrine was correct. Often if a person gave a wrong answer or made a wrong "confession" they were quickly corrected. As a result, they were not very successful in attracting either unbelievers or new believers to their groups. This was a huge problem because the small group program was one of the main discipleship arms of the church.

And now these three remain: faith, hope and love. But the greatest of these is love.

1 Corinthians 13:13

We asked the pastor for his blessing to change the entire small group culture, which he readily gave. We explained that there were two main values represented by the small group program: discipleship and fellowship. And when it came to a conflict between the two, discipleship always prevailed, thus, the "doctrine/confession police." The small group program

63

had unintentionally taken 1 Corinthians 13:13 and changed it to: "...the greatest of these is *faith*."

We all realized that this needed to change – that we needed to make the groups more relationally focused. We recognized that our people didn't need more teaching because the pastor was such a strong teacher. They needed relational connection. We even wrote an entire years' worth of discussion guides to help the small group leaders catch the heart of what we were trying to accomplish with their groups. *(These are available as a free download from our website.*[60] *)*

We began to retrain the leaders, imparting the new DNA and modeling for them what we wanted to see in the groups. It was quite messy at first, and we lost some solid leaders because the new style wasn't what they wanted. But God sent us a new crop of leaders/hosts. They, along with the current leaders that were willing to adjust, breathed new life into the program. We found it quite easy to get new believers involved. Even some unchurched people were willing to come. It was because the groups weren't focused on telling people what they were doing wrong or needed to do. They were more about sharing our stories, our hopes and fears, and on celebrating how God and the Bible were changing our lives. We focused on truly connecting with others, not making sure their answers or doctrine were correct. A fringe benefit was that we now attracted leaders that earlier didn't feel theologically qualified to lead a group.

A breakthrough for us came when we discovered that it was okay to leave questions unanswered. Or we at least allowed others in the group to share conflicting viewpoints, as long as it was done in a respectful way. If no one else came to what we considered to be a doctrinally correct viewpoint, we often briefly shared relevant Bible verses and our take on the subject matter, and then invited further discussion. The point wasn't to correct them, but allow people to learn from each other; and in doing so, experience true biblical community.

Actually Robin and I had the privilege of leading a Bible study that was focused on the unchurched, especially those that were just investigating Christianity. The culture of this group was one of welcome and genuine acceptance. Because of this we had drug dealers, high priced corporate "escorts," atheists and addicts involved... some of them were drunk or stoned every time they came. This was because the small group host was very active in the community, and because we intentionally made the group an open place of acceptance and sharing. It was exciting to see people make commitments to Christ and to watch lives begin to change for the better!

Culture Matters!

It's been said that culture trumps everything. Culture is the *ethos* of an organization – its underlying and often unspoken DNA. It is rarely articulated, but rather felt. It is like a movie soundtrack in that it sets the mood and intensity level. Many churches have great vision/mission statements and core values listed on their walls and websites, but where they invest their finances, focus and best leaders doesn't match their stated values and vision. More than anything else an organization's *culture* will determine its direction and what it actually becomes. When a church's vision, core values and culture are aligned the sky is the limit!

The Perrin family culture is probably quite strange to many people – we are loud and brutally honest, yet encouraging; and we love to make each other laugh (we truly have a quirky sense of humor). We love all kinds of movies. As a matter of fact, one of our favorite games is to try to "out-quote" each other with movie lines. ("One-liners" from family movies are our specialty.) We can try to act refined and "perfect," but it won't last long because that's not really who we are. Why? Authenticity is part of our family culture.

In the same way, a church's culture determines what it will become. It is just as important as the core values because it sets the trajectory of the church. It goes far beyond the written vision statement that declares what we want to be. It determines who we as a church really are, and how we are uniquely created to glorify God.

Because we planted a new church, we were able to create the culture from scratch. The Watermark culture was birthed in our hearts through prayer. It was one of serving and celebration, inclusion and giving, excellence and leadership development. No matter what we said, our culture was the most significant determining factor in who we became as a church. And we learned that we had to continually model and impart our DNA into the people God called to serve alongside us.

We've seen many churches that recognize the need to engage younger generations, not just in youth or college ministries but also in the "main" service. In response pastors often only tweak external things like ditching their coats and ties, installing intelligent lighting and fog machines, sitting on a barstool or updating the style of music. But unless the actual *culture* of the church and the attitude of the leadership is overhauled, to the unchurched it seems more like Grandpa sporting new pair of skinny jeans. It's inauthentic and awkward, and it just doesn't work.

When it comes to culture, it doesn't matter what you say about your church, your actions will always speak louder than words. For instance, many churches claim to be child-friendly, but give them worn out facilities and toys, and have no budget for training the Kids Church volunteers. It really only takes minutes for people to determine if your stated values are true or not.

I used to ask our first time visitors if they could tell what we truly valued at Watermark. Most of them could name at least three of our core values. Why? We talked about them often and we organized our church around them. We'll talk more about values in the next chapter and in the chapters on Alignment.

Pastors that take over or change existing churches need to patiently impart the new DNA and culture they want to see into their people. An established church's culture won't change overnight. It will take time and effort. But the results are worth it!

"Leaders often underestimate the power of an entrenched set of values and behaviors – that's what culture is."[61]

If you want your church culture to change you need to starve the wrong beliefs and actions and feed the right ones. To starve the wrong beliefs, look for organizational actions that run contrary to your core values. Once you've identified the wrong actions, look for the corresponding wrong beliefs such as:

- Meeting my goals is my number one priority. (Numbers matter most.)

- My area of ministry has to succeed or I'll lose my job.

- There aren't enough good volunteers to go around.

- Filling a hole is more important than positioning someone according to their strengths.

- If I don't keep (insert volunteer's name) my team won't like me.

- It can't be done.

Confront the wrong behaviors with the person responsible. Try to be as positive as possible. You want them to learn from this conversation, not be crushed by it. Help them see how the action goes against the core values. Then work with them to determine the wrong belief behind the action, and the right belief.

Next, you need to decide how to best counter the false beliefs with cultural values. Teach them to your leaders, and set an expectation for them to embody these beliefs in their teams. The best way to reinforce your church's values is to:

- **Pray it out.** Pray it out with your church and your leaders. Our prayers show our people what is important enough to bring before God. When we pray out the vision with passion our people catch our heart. And when God begins to answer these prayers our people see that it's *God's* dream, not just *ours*!

- **Say it often.** Make it a part of your sermons and your announcements. As Dr. Gerald Brooks says, "Put a face on the vision." Tell real life stories of how the vision is working. Peter Drucker famously said, "Churches are in the business of changed lives." When our leaders and our churches see real life results from the new vision the overall culture will begin to change.

- **Display it openly.** If you want your people to do it, you have to model it before them. You need to first prove to them that it works, not just on paper, but also in the real world. If you tell your people that you're going to try it together you may end up doing it alone. Pastor Scott Wilson of The Oaks Fellowship in Dallas said he began *personally* implementing a personal growth plan a full year before challenging his staff to join him.[62]

- **Reward it publicly.** *(Sorry, I'm obviously not as cool as those preachers that can make EVERYTHING rhyme or match; but if I were, this bullet point would probably be, "Prize it outwardly")* Celebrate results! What you reward gets repeated. You reward it by telling success stories of your people from the pulpit or in your advertising. Or you could send a handwritten note of appreciation. Even a phone call, an email or a text message telling them how proud you are of them will make a difference. The main thing is to celebrate people taking steps toward the vision.

Chapter 9
Who Am I?

The *process* of discovering God's plan for your church is the same as that of discovering His plan for your life. You need to wait on Him and take steps in the direction of where you feel He is leading you. If it's not right, you'll know soon enough. But before you announce it to your church you need to give yourself time to process it thoroughly and make sure you have an actionable plan, or at least a clear direction to head toward. The best thing to do would be to pray it out with a few people that have a common heart and passion.

When God first spoke to us about planting a church we prayed A LOT. We wanted to have a basic idea of what it should look like before talking with anyone about it. After the picture became a little clearer in our hearts we talked with our Perrin Ministries Board of Directors, my pastor and some friends we greatly respect. We also talked with the pastors at the church we were attending. We wanted their input. Even though we were sure we had heard from God we wanted to get some insight from people that knew us well. If they'd had concerns, we would have prayed more before moving forward. They all gave us their blessing, so we took the next step.

(I do need to add, embarrassingly, a great piece of great advice from my pastor that I failed to heed. He told me I needed to have a hundred thousand dollars in the bank before I launched the church. I just **knew** *that the money would come in, so I ignored his wisdom.* **[DUMB MOVE!]** *Unfortunately, it caught up with us!* **Two loans later** *our church was doing well. But we were stuck paying back loans that we never should have gotten. But let me say that while we do need to first "count the*

cost"[63] before jumping in, we can't let the amount of money we raise be the determining factor as to whether or not we obey the Holy Spirit.)

In church planter training I was taught that you start off determining who you DON'T want to be as a church. After seeking God and thinking through what that could look like you eventually realize who you DO want to be. This is exactly the way it was in our case. Many of the protestant churches in Freiburg were fairly similar to one another, with the same music, the same style of ministry, the same stage setup, etc. There was one church in town that was more "current" in its style, but it still didn't look like what we had in our hearts.

We knew we needed to offer a fresh style of church service, one that was welcoming and accessible to the unchurched. Many people call this being "seeker-sensitive." We didn't like this because of the baggage that phrase carries with it. God gave us the term "user friendly." To put it in geek speak, we wanted to be a *Mac* church in a *DOS* world.

Bringing Your Leaders Along With You

You should always begin sharing your vision (or making any changes) by getting your leaders on board. Leadership expert Dr. John Maxwell calls this The Law Of The Buy-In. I can't stress enough the vital importance of having your leaders in your corner before moving forward. Make sure your people are in alignment (vastly different than "agreement") first. We'll cover this topic in more detail in the chapters on Alignment. We started praying, dreaming and planning with an ever-growing team of amazing people eight months before we launched.

We would take our Launch Team to visit other churches in town to see if what they were *actually doing* in their services lined up with their *stated vision and core values*. Then we would talk about how their vision and values differed from ours. This was incredibly productive in our Launch Team training! It enabled us to get a clearer picture of who God had created *us* to be. And it showed us the importance of making sure everyone on our Launch Team had our God-given DNA in their hearts.

Pastor Matt Keller of Next Level Church in Ft. Meyers, FL likes to say that we all have a different setting in mind when asked to draw a picture of the sunset. Some envision a dock overlooking a calm lake with the sun disappearing on the horizon. Others imagine rolling hills, a meadow, the beach or a mountain in front of the setting sun. But when it comes to planting a church we need to all see the same picture. Our job as leaders is to paint that sunset in such a way that our people can picture the same sunset we envision before we move ahead.

Questions We Must Answer

As you pray out God's thumbprint for your church, you need to answer a few basic questions:

- **What** are we called to do? (This is your mission.)

- **Where** are we going? (This is your vision.)

- **Why** are we doing it? (These are your core values.)

- **Who** are we called to serve? (This is your target audience.)

- **How** are we going to do it? (This is your strategy.)

- **When** are we going to do it? (These are your goals.)

The *where* was really the first one from this list that God revealed to us: "To be a church for those that don't do church." But for us the most important question was the *why*. This gave us our core values (which are listed in the first chapter of this book). Without the *why* the rest of the questions would make no sense, nor would there be any passion behind the answers. As we prayed over our four core values we discovered the answers to the rest of these questions.

Our core values also helped us stay focused. They streamlined everything we did. Because a church plant has limited resources it has to be wise in where they are invested. Your core values will help you make these decisions quickly and with confidence. When someone came to us with an idea that they wanted our church to do the first question we asked them was, "How does this fit with our core values?" If it didn't fit, we encouraged the person to find a ministry that was already doing this and partner with them. We made no apologies for who God had called us to be.

These two illustrations below describe the effect of having a unified picture of the sunset. Without a unified vision (*Figure 1*) we end up pulling in opposite directions. It's much the same as a car stuck in the mud – its wheels spin but there is no forward motion. But when we are all unified and pulling in the same direction (*Figure 2*), the full force of our energy is applied, giving us maximum results from our efforts.

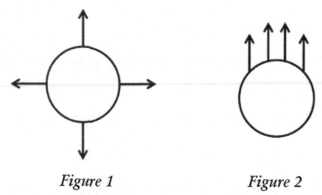

Figure 1   *Figure 2*

Put Your Money Where Your Mouth Is

One time the person that was scheduled to translate Robin in Kids Church informed us on Saturday morning that she couldn't serve the next day because she was sick. I could have given my message in either English or German, but not both; and since we were a bilingual church we needed translation. Only one other person from our translation team was in town at the time, and she was actually scheduled to translate for me in the adult service. Robin told me, "I guess that means I get *your* translator tomorrow." I protested, but she replied, "Put your money where your mouth is. You say that kids are a core value… this is your chance to prove it."

That was PAINFUL! But she was right. It's one thing to have a written list of core values. It's another to make painful choice because of them. Your values make your choices for you. They predetermine the priority of the decisions that we have to make (spending, staffing, scheduling, etc.). If we don't have our core values settled we will end up choosing the option that causes the least friction, or even worse, the one promoted by the strongest-willed person with the loudest voice. You have to fight for your vision and values.

To resolve the story, when faced with a sick translator we asked our Launch Team for creative solutions to our predicament and one of them volunteered to translate. He ended up translating for Robin and did an outstanding job. He later became a valuable member of our translation team.

During our church planting journey Robin and I quickly realized what we'd been told many times, that there is a constant inertia which attempts to bring the focus back onto the people that already occupy the church seats, instead of on the unchurched or de-churched people that haven't walked in through the doors yet. Rob Ketterling, Lead Pastor of River Valley Church in Apple Valley, MN area was right when he told a group of European leaders, "If the lost are going to have a voice in my church, it has to be mine." We knew we needed to constantly keep the vision in front of our people.

We had a talented young couple that agreed to join our Launch Team a few months before we started. He was gifted with his hands and had an entrepreneurial business mind, and she could have run the church by herself. But it seemed as if they wanted to bring everything back to focusing ministry on *our* people. Since they had a passion for "house churches" it stands to reason that they wanted to maintain the small, cozy family feel. But God clearly told us to put our focus on those *outside* of our church. We had poured so much vision concerning our God-given target audience – the unchurched and de-churched – into our Launch Team members that this couple's ideas never gained any traction. If we hadn't spent so much time and energy filling our Team with the vision God gave us this couple might have gained enough influence to hijack it, albeit unintentionally.

Many churches we have coached talked about reaching the lost but didn't train their people to do so and did no intentional outreach. Understandably they didn't see many visitors. Their core value of being evangelistic or of reaching people far from

God was only a nice sentiment. What a church really values is revealed by where they invest the greatest percentage of their strategy, their resources and their best people. If it's a core value, then it's something worth fighting for. And it has to be modeled by the leadership because it flows from the top down.

Why Do We Exist?

When people come to church for the first time they bring a lot of baggage (just as we all do). But what would a church be like that actually *invited* people to bring all their problems, questions and doubts? Where they could **belong** *before* they **believe**? Wouldn't *that* be a church that attracted the unchurched? Doesn't that sound like a church where you could experience Jesus without having to wade through all the fluff, hypocrisy and shame? This was exactly the type of church we were supposed to be!

Many retailers have forgotten to inform their employees of their true purpose. A cashier isn't there to simply ring up purchases and to do so as quickly and efficiently as possible. He has been hired to ensure his customers have a good shopping experience and are able to leave with their purchases as soon as they're finished. But it often appears that grocery store cashiers seem to think – or maybe they're told – that it's their job to shove the groceries down the line and into the bag as soon as possible. Heaven forbid that they should actually have to have a conversation with the customer.

A teacher's main purpose is to teach students how gather relevant facts and information and apply them practically. It's to help her students learn to think creatively. Sadly, some teachers act as if they exist simply to transfer knowledge of facts and information to their students. The teachers we remember are the ones that made learning fun, or at least interesting... those that sparked our curiosity.

In the same way, too many churches have forgotten their purpose. We exist to reach outsiders with the message of God's grace. Jesus' stated mission was, "to seek and save the lost."[64] Then He handed the baton off to us: "Go into all the world and preach the Gospel to every nation."[65] As Pastor

Randy Ayers of Cross Mountain Church in Boerne, TX says, "Churches aren't to be refuges *from* the world, but refuges *for* the world."

So many church leaders have bought into the lie that their church exists to have good services. Unfortunately, because so many churches believe this they tend to focus inward, on keeping their current members content. The natural human tendency is to form a closed circle of relationships. In churches this "inbreeding" produces spiritually deformed Christ-followers, just like natural inbreeding does to offspring. It leaves no room for the outsiders God has called us to reach.

So many of our church members feel the church is there to meet *their personal needs*, and that of their families. This is NOT why we exist! This is not the Church that Jesus died to establish. It is not the goal for which He trained His disciples.

On the contrary, churches exist to bring hope into a hopeless world. Jesus reminded His disciples that, "You are the light of the world."[66] The Apostle Paul writes that people without God have no hope.[67] Genuine life-giving hope is one thing the Church can offer that people can't find anywhere else.

We never allowed our church to forget their primary mission: to help the unchurched and de-churched connect with God and with each other, and to help those that are serving God find a place to use their gifts to build the Kingdom.

Target Audience

I want to take a moment and drill down on this point a little more. Although we want to reach every person that is far from God, each church is more likely to connect with a certain group of people. They make up our target audience. Even though God is not limited by our circumstances, most churches operate with limited resources so they need to be invested wisely. We need to discover our ministry sweet spot – the people we are most likely to reach. If we put most of our finances, time and energy into this area we will see the greatest payoff.

At our church it was crystal clear that we were called to

reach the unchurched. We assumed that this would be people that had no connection with church whatsoever. And we did reach quite a few from this people group in Freiburg. But our greatest results were with the "de-churched," those that had been involved in a church but had walked away. As a matter of fact, this group made up about 60% of our people at one point. Initially I felt this was a failure to reach the ones I considered to be our target audience. But after reading Andy Stanley's book *Deep & Wide,* I realized that this group was also unchurched. They had decided never to go to church again – they were simply *done* with church. God sent us many "dones" so we could lead them to Christ (or *back* to Christ) and disciple them.

One quick note about the dones that we know… most of them had been committed to a church but ended up feeling abused, ignored or otherwise taken advantage of. Many were simply funneled into an area of ministry in service of the church, but it ended up feeling more like indentured servitude. They were simply warm bodies filling a hole in the organizational chart, having been given no vision or passion for the task they were assigned. They brought ideas and heart, yet were rebuffed with "that's not how we do it here."

Chapter 10
Why Churches Fail

Pastors of dwindling churches are often unwilling to change, even though it is obvious their church is struggling. They double down on what has worked for them in the past, using excuses like, "Those people that left weren't really committed anyway," as if *they* should be more interested in the Church. In reality, though, Christ called His Church to be interested in *them!*[68]

When faced with decline many churches take steps to stop the bleeding, but never do the hard work of discovering and solving the underlying problems. They go into damage control/maintenance mode, trying not to lose any more people. But this is only a temporary fix – a patch, if you will. It won't resolve the issue. As a matter of fact, it will end up frustrating or hurting your best leaders because the defensive measures that you put in place will end up tying their hands. Good leaders move forward, even in times of crisis. If the organization prevents them from moving forward they will look for another church where they *are* able to make progress.

Some pastors with the same spiritual background as Robin and me believe the answer is to be *more spiritual*, and to seek more "signs and wonders." Don't get me wrong... we have seen God do amazing things – spectacular supernatural miracles – and we believe in the power of the Living God! Unfortunately, this is not a "Get Out of Jail Free" card that will solve all of your church's problems. My question is, if prayer alone were going to grow our churches and reach our cities why aren't our churches growing or our cities being reached? Most churches don't fail because of lack of prayer or passion. They fail because of the lack of a clear vision.

Some churches are strong in discipleship, others in evangelism, worship or relationships. But in order for you to fulfill God's destiny for your church you need to determine your God-given DNA and then adjust your *style* to connect to the culture around you. It's important to note that the pastor's personality will drive the church's style, to some extent. But that can't be an excuse to continue doing what you've always done because it's easier than changing the way you do things.

You need to continually evaluate your effectiveness in each of the core value areas God has given you. This is even more important to analyze if your church is well established. The longer a church has been in existence, the greater the chance it has experienced (or is currently experiencing) mission drift.

You need to be willing to get on your face before God until you catch His vision for your church, even if you've been in ministry for 30 years. What worked at your last church probably won't work at this one. What Saddleback Church, Willow Creek Church or even Watermark Church has done won't work for you either, unless God Himself tells you to do it. You can't make a packaged set of core values, mission, vision and strategy work for your church, although you *can* learn the principles and best practices that have worked for other churches.

Many pastors read Rick Warren's *Purpose-Driven Church* and come to the conclusion that their core values need to be the five purposes of church. Or they hear Bill Hybels speak and say, "We need to be more like Willow Creek Church." Some pastors would rather be trendy, but they will only have a one-generational church.

These are all good starting points. But God's unique thumbprint for your church needs to come from Him, not the leader of an influential megachurch. The reason that megachurch *is* so big and influential is that they received a DNA download from God Himself and ran with it.

Maybe borrowing someone else's vision and strategy *is* what God is telling you to do. That's not the norm. If copying another church's vision isn't working for you let me suggest that the principles in this book may be the reason why. You need to study the relevant cultural shifts and your local/regional demographics and culture around you, and then be willing to adjust your style.

We've had pastors tell us, "If we change, we'll lose some people." That is absolutely true! Dr. Gerald Brooks says that you grow a church by choosing whom you're willing to lose. At Watermark we were willing to lose "professional Christians" – those that simply take up space on a Sunday. They feed off the energy of the services but never add anything or get involved anywhere. This is okay for people just checking out the church. But we expected more from those that called our church "home" (those who had been with us awhile). We were not content to be a consumer church. We invited and expected everyone to get involved in some way.

As we said, it's important to know your target audience and adjust to reach them. But know that other demographic groups probably won't connect as well with your style. If your music is young, loud and hip you shouldn't expect to reach the older generation. If you don't offer children's ministry you shouldn't expect to reach young families. Likewise, if you don't offer youth ministry you probably won't see many established families in attendance.

You also need to remember that people visit a church based on a need they either have or perceive. By meeting that need you will be able to connect with them. The trouble comes when we try to meet *every* need. This is exhausting and will keep you from seeing your vision come to pass. Let me give you a secret to avoiding burnout: You need to remember that you are not the Savior. You are not called to meet every need. You are called to do your part, and to trust God to do the rest.

Besides, when you say yes to something, you're saying no to something else. We need to say no to the wrong things – even though they may actually be good things – so we can say yes to the right things. Your resources (time, energy, focus, finances, staff, volunteers, influence, etc.) are limited, so it's imperative that you prioritize where you will invest them.

I want to add that hiring a good church consultant might also be a wise thing to do. He or she can help you connect the dots in the DNA discovery process. But remember that not everyone who says he or she is a consultant is going to benefit your church. Be sure to find one that has a proven track record in helping churches in your context (size, style, region, etc.).

How To Determine Your God-Given DNA

When it comes to determining your church's God-given DNA, the very first step is to spend as much time as needed seeking God's heart. As you do, you might consider these questions:

- **Who has God called together for this organization?** (If you don't have anyone with musical gifts, it's likely that music/worship won't be one of your core values.)

- **What keeps our team members awake at night? What do they dream about? What are they passionate about?** (Pastor Bill Hybels calls this your "Holy Discontent.")

- **What needs are in our community/context?** (Remember: Jesus met practical needs in the lives of those that followed Him.) God places churches in settings where so they can impact their communities. The best way to impact a community is to meet felt needs.

Once you've discovered the answers to these questions, look for patterns, connections and similarities. Often you can discover God's thumbprint at the intersection of your team members' shared dreams, passions and gifting and the needs of the community.

As you begin to get a general sense of your mission, vision and/or values you'll need to boil each one down to its irreducible minimum. Your mission and vision statements and core values need to be portable and repeatable (i.e. short and clear). You want your members to be able to quickly and accurately share what makes your church worth attending, and what makes it different from the other churches in town.

For Watermark, we knew from the beginning that we were called to reach outsiders, especially a younger audience. We played around with different vision statements, such as, "A new way to do church" and "Not your momma's church." But it became clear that these didn't really have any "teeth" to them. They defined who we didn't want to be (and suggested that we were better than other churches). We needed to define who we DID want to be – who God was calling us to be.

We landed on "a church for the unchurched," but knew that this phrase was still a bit odd for our German culture. We prayed some more and kicked it around until we came up with "A church for those that don't do church." That's pretty clear. It defined both our focus and our target audience.

As we prayed out what this could look like, our core values began to take shape. We looked at a long list of values, but settled on four (listed in the first chapter of this book). As we began to dream together with our team we worked on defining our cultural values. The more steps we took in the direction of our dream the clearer it became. And writing our dreams, ideas and thoughts down on paper helped us to visually connect the dots in different areas of ministry. It helped us create our strategy. As you can see, it is helpful to have both visionary and strategically gifted leaders to help with this process.

We have included some diagnostic questions and resources for this and the rest of the core components on the http://PostChristianTsunami.com website.

Discussion Questions:

Why is a church's culture so important? How can you change an organization's culture?

Why do you think churches resist change?

What are you core values? What are your cultural values?

Who has God created your church to be? What has He called you to do? Who has He specifically called you to reach? How will you accomplish what He's called you to do?

What spiritual or natural gifts has God given to your team members? How are you leveraging them in your church?

ACCESSIBILITY

Welcoming The World With Open Arms

Churches are uncomfortably odd places for an unchurched person. The language, traditions, customs and even the people seem just plain weird. What happens in most churches on a Sunday has little to do with life in the real world on a Monday.

Additionally, pastors often refer to unchurched people as "unsaved," "lost," or my personal favorite: "sinners" in their sermons. Because of the inclusive nature of Post-Christian society – especially among Millennials – this *us versus them mentality* may cost you the opportunity of reaching the unreached. How would you feel if people around you talked about you as if you weren't even there?

We *must* change this! We have to make our churches more user-friendly, inviting and welcoming. We will have to be intentional if we want to connect with an increasingly secular society. We have to consciously take an introspective look at our churches and try to see them through the eyes of a person that has never been to a church before, or may be giving the Church one last chance. If we can learn to see through their eyes we can begin to make our churches welcoming environments where people can truly "come as you are."

Chapter 11
What A Church Should Look Like

"The church is the one institution that exists for the benefit of those who are not yet members."

William Temple, Archbishop of Canterbury

Spiritual leaders cannot afford to give in to the consumer mindset of future generations. When ministering to Millennials, our tendency is to ask them what they want. This won't always work. Many unchurched Millennials don't know how to put into words what they want or need. And besides, catering to their whims would only screw up a church.

But at the same time, we also can't continue to keep doing business as usual. We know that in its purest form the Gospel *is* offensive. It confronts the small-minded, selfish lifestyle we've accepted as normal. Jesus regularly had people walk away. But if people are going to be offended in our churches it should be because of the *message*, not because of the *messengers*. Often churches unintentionally do things that scare away the very visitors they seek to attract.

Too many churches are focused on insiders, yet wonder why they can't attract or retain outsiders. The solution is easier than you would think, but it requires a lot of introspection, intentionality and courage.

What a Visitor Fears
Can you remember back to the first time you visited a church? Do you remember how scary it was? We need to be

sensitive to an unchurched visitor's fears when visiting a church:

- I'll stand out, or be singled out and embarrassed.

- I won't fit in. I'll feel like an outsider.

- I won't know what to do or what to say.

- Everyone will look down on me.

- I'll be made to feel guilty and ashamed because I'm not perfect.

- What if I don't believe it? I just can't believe like they do... it's not that easy for me. Besides, what the preacher says probably won't make sense to me anyway.

- I'll probably be the only one who doesn't know how to find something in the Bible. And if I don't bring a Bible *everyone* will notice.

- This church only wants my money!

Be sure to read about our experiences as church visitors on the Post-Christian Tsunami Blog under the title, "We are Visitors."[69]

What Church Looks Like To a Visitor

As we said in the last chapter, the unchurched visit a church because they have a need in their life. They usually don't just wake up early one beautiful Sunday morning and say, "I'm going to go to church today." No. Pastor Carey Nieuwhof says that the unchurched think about visiting a church as often as a Christian thinks about visiting a synagogue – rarely, if ever.

Unchurched people visit churches because they realize something in their life isn't right. It may be an external situation like divorce, financial crisis, chronic sickness or family problems. Or it may just be due to curiosity driven by a gnawing soul hunger. A person that visits your church is either looking for something or has a lot of trust in the person that invited them.

If God actually answered our prayers and sent the unchurched – especially people far from God – to *our* churches, what would they experience? In many churches they wouldn't be drawn to God but rather freaked out. Most of them would be *repelled* from God rather than *attracted* to Him because of the odd rituals and traditions they would find. You may think that your church doesn't have rituals or traditions but every church does – we've just accepted these things as "normal." Unfortunately, many of these traditions seem weird to people that aren't familiar with them.

We would like to believe that our churches aren't ritualistic or tradition-bound, but they most certainly are. In our services our greeters, music, announcements and preaching have a certain style and rhythm. Even the style/appearance of our meeting facility creates a part of our culture. This isn't necessarily wrong. On the contrary, these are all a part of our local church culture, which makes our church distinct from other churches. Whether it is Baptist, Catholic, Charismatic, Methodist, Presbyterian or non-denominational, every church/denomination has its own style.

The problem is that many of us have forgotten what church looks like to a visitor. If we're going to address their fears, we must discover what *they* see and how our churches make *them* feel. Church looks VERY different to a visitor than it does to a member. It's even more unfamiliar to a *totally* unchurched person, which we hope to see more of in the future.

Our recent visit to a local church is a perfect example of this. When the worship team finished they encouraged people to greet each other. Robin sat down as the pastor came to the pulpit, which was normal for every other church we've attended. A lady behind us tapped her on the shoulder and politely said to her, "We stand for the reading of the Word in our church." I understand where she is coming from… really, I do. She was probably just trying to be helpful. But had we been *unchurched* visitors – especially if we had NEVER been in a church before – we would probably have left **right then**! She could have chosen her words better, or at least waited until after the service to try to be helpful. Robin would have certainly figured it out when she was the only one sitting down as the pastor started. But in this instance the conversation was more embarrassing than helpful.

So what does a visitor experience?

Strange customs (with no explanation) – It might as well be a secret handshake that only members know. When we don't explain why we do what we do in our services it makes visitors ask questions like: "Why does everyone stand up for the singing? Why does everyone 'greet one another' before the preacher speaks? Why do they 'encourage' me to give in the offering? *I knew they just wanted my money!*"

Many pastors and believers that come from the same spiritual background as Robin and I do are focused on having the spiritual gifts as listed in 1 Corinthians 12 active in their services. Some of these pastors feel that if these "signs and wonders" are not present in every church service, their church is "backslidden." The Apostle Paul dealt with this same attitude in one of the churches he planted. Thankfully his instruction to them was written down so we, too, can benefit from it.

> *"I enter into this [praying in tongues] as much or more than any of you. But when I'm in a church assembled for worship, I'd rather say five words that everyone can understand and learn from than say ten thousand that sound to others like gibberish."*
>
> *1 Corinthians 14:18-19 MSG*

It's not that we are embarrassed or want to avoid this proof that God's Spirit is actively at work in our services. We'd rather focus on those things that help the unchurched and those not familiar with our customs to understand what God is doing. Robin and I learned to quickly explain anything out of the ordinary in our services so that those unfamiliar with such things wouldn't be freaked out. Besides, the Book of Acts indicates that most of the time such signs and wonders were manifested *outside* of a church service in order to get the attention of unbelievers.

Even weirder language (also with no explanation) – How is an unchurched visitor – especially one with absolutely no Christian background – supposed to understand church terms like righteousness, holiness, salvation and hallelujah? Many pastors use the phrase, "Who you are in Christ." But what does that mean to a person who is visiting a church for the first time? Worship leaders often use phrases like "Sing a new song to the Lord," as if a visitor is supposed to know how to do that. Even when it's spoken with a pure heart, this so-called "God talk" can chase off visitors!

We need to use *inclusive* language in our churches. This means we should avoid words that create a sense of *us* and *them* (insiders versus outsiders), referring to people that are far from God as "sinners" or "unsaved," or even as "lost." Even though these may be Bible terms, they don't connect with the people we are called to reach. On the contrary, these words can make them feel like *even more* of an outsider. Our language needs to be inclusive and welcoming!

For instance, when talking about sin I tell unchurched people that I realize they may have some hang-ups with that word. I take time to define it in everyday terms and then share how it will damage our lives. I always finish by sharing how Jesus delivered us from it and that we can overcome it.

Embarrassment – As we've already said, one of the biggest fears a visitor has is to be embarrassed in church. Asking them to stand and introduce themselves, or sometimes even to simply raise their hand, can be terrifying and play to this fear. We've found it's far better to have them fill out a visitor card and drop it off at the Info Booth. The advantage to this is that *they* are choosing to give you their contact information and to be placed on your mailing list. Marketing guru Seth Godin says getting people to "opt in" – voluntarily sign up to be contacted – dramatically increases their willingness to actually receive what you desire to communicate with them.

Insider jokes – Another thing that frustrates visitors is when the pastor makes jokes that refer to one of the members. Of course the visitor doesn't get the joke, even though church members may find it hysterical. This just reinforces the feeling that the visitor is an outsider. It is about the same as if you were the new kid in a high school and sat down at a lunch table full of students. How would you feel if one of them made a joke that everyone but you laughed at, and they never bothered to explain it to you?

In some churches, the Kids Church service is not good – WE BELIEVE IT IS A SIN TO BORE KIDS IN CHURCH! This is not representative of God's heart. If we want to reach young families we have to offer a fun experience for their kids. And the unfortunate truth is that if you don't reach young families your church will eventually die out.

If you don't have a strong Kids Church team we have some suggestions for you:

- Pray that God would send you some good people. God knows what you need. He's the one that said, "Everything is possible to those that believe."[70] Because celebrating kids was one of our core values we trusted that God would send us the necessary people for it... and He did! We would not have launched the church without quality people in our Kids Church area.

- When you find someone with suitable gifts and a passion for kids, ask them to check out the Kids Church for a couple of weeks. *Of course you need to do a background check first.* Follow up with them each time they visit the Kids Church. If they show interest ask them to commit to serving for a trial period. We asked our Kids Church team members to commit for three months initially. Then if that went well we asked them for a six-month or one-year commitment.

- Even though you will probably need to start by searching for someone that loves kids, as your ministry grows you need to look for someone who can develop others. You are best off not settling for a "worker" to lead this area of ministry. You should look for leaders, those that can train others to lead and serve.

- The complaint I hear most often from Kids Church workers is that they feel *stuck*. To them it seems as if the leaders are simply looking to fill holes in the organizational chart. To many of them it seems the leaders don't care whether or not a person has to serve three or four weeks in a row. All that matters is finding "babysitters" so the adult ministry can go forward. *This is not okay... not even a little bit!* It doesn't matter what pastors say, perception is reality. If your workers are frustrated that they have to serve in Kids Church they will end up taking it out on the kids. And yes, we believe it is okay to pay your Kids Church and Nursery workers, if necessary.

- Give your Kids Church team the resources and training they need. There are lots of low-cost Kids Church resources out there. Most of your Kids Church workers aren't able to commit the time necessary to develop a lesson, a story, a craft and a game each week. Giving them pre-packaged lesson plans is a great way to let them know you want them to succeed. Give them permission to adjust the lesson, as necessary. Just make sure you give it to them early enough for them to come prepared for the service.

- Support the teachers/workers. Kids Church workers are often the least appreciated people in the church. This is sad. They need to know that their efforts matter. Every time you hear of a positive story concerning the Kids Church, be sure to share it with the church and ask your members to thank the workers when they see them. If the pastor regularly casts vision for Kids Church he/she will have a constant supply of good people ready to serve in that area.

- Never put a person in Kids Church that is a "disciplinarian." Your kids will get a wrong picture of who God is! We believe that kids should be celebrated in church, that every child is a superstar – even those that Geni Brooks, the Children's Pastor of Grace Outreach Center in Plano, TX, calls EGRs (Extra Grace Required). One time we needed some more Kids Church workers as a result of a staff change, and the only person we could find at the time didn't like kids very much. So Robin and I took turns serving in Kids Church at that point. Even though there were other areas of the church that needed our attention, our kids were a priority and we treated them as such.

- Robin wrote an excellent series of 13 blog posts called, "Thoughts on Children's Ministry." You can find it on our Perrin Ministries Leadership Blog.[71] This is great material for training your Kids Church team!

The Welcome Factor

"I'd rather have a welcoming church than a friendly church. The welcoming church is always thinking guests first. They expect new people to show up every week. They are intentional about how they greet and welcome those guests. They are intentional about how they communicate, worship and teach with guests in their services. Friendly churches, on the other hand, can be some of the most unwelcoming places in the world, because the focus is on people who already are part of the church."[72]

Tony Morgan

If we don't *intentionally* look at our churches through the eyes of a visitor, we won't notice things that need to change. Your "welcome factor" includes all the things a visitor notices when he/she comes. This can make or break your first impression. While people won't notice things such as the sound or how clean or orderly the building is when things are functioning well, they MOST CERTAINLY will notice if things are not right.

In our house when the kids come home after work or school they kick off their shoes, drop their backpacks and other assorted stuff, take off their jackets, etc… *our house looks lived in.* We expect them to keep the house orderly, but we don't follow them around with a broom or a vacuum. On special occasions like Christmas or Thanksgiving when lots of company is coming over we do, however, make sure things are not only straightened, but also very clean. Even our kids' rooms are expected to be clean and orderly. We are not aiming for "sterile," but rather for neat and clean. It shows our guests that we are *expecting* them to come, and that we want their experience at our house to be a pleasant one.

Your church's welcome factor consists of things such as:

The condition of the building – Is the lawn kept neat and clean? What about the parking lot? Is the building dirty or in need of repair or a fresh coat of paint? Are there water stains, dirt, mold or cobwebs in the building? *(One of our pet peeves is a dirty/messy/smelly bathroom!)* Is the stage cluttered or disorganized (i.e. instrument cases or extra music stands lying around or the microphone cables looking like a plate of spaghetti)? Is the sound booth/table neat and orderly, or does it look more like a teenager's bedroom? What about the Kids Church rooms? Are they clean, neat and inviting; or are they messy and chaotic, looking more like a storage closet – or worse, a janitor's closet – than a safe, inviting and fun atmosphere where kids are cared for and taught?

Signage – Why is signage important? Again, everything they see says something about your church and its culture.

- If they can't find the church or the parking lot because there is no signage near the road;

- If the front entrance, restrooms, auditorium, classrooms, Kids Church/nursery rooms, Visitor Info Booth and exits aren't clearly labeled;

- And if the signs they *do* see look more like quickly hand-drawn garage sale signs,

… you are making a clear statement: "We don't know what we're doing." You are expecting a visitor to simply *know* where these things are. But how can they if they've never been to your church? What would a grocery store with no signs be like? And even worse, what if there was no one to help a person find the grocery items she needed? It would be more like an *inconvenience* store! That store wouldn't stay in business very long!

Preparedness of the Team – Everything should be totally prepared *before* any visitors arrive. At our church we required all pre-service preparations to be finished by 10:00 am so we could hang out as a team for a few minutes before our pre-service meeting, which started at 10:15 am. Although our service started at 11:00 am people started arriving 30 minutes earlier. When visitors arrived our entire focus was on *them*. After everyone left, most of our Team hung out, drank coffee and had snacks or lunch together.

We need to avoid giving off the impression that this is our first rodeo. There is nothing that says "rookie" like a volunteer unlocking the Kids Church room and turning on the lights and heating *after* the service is supposed to begin. *(Yes, we actually experienced this in a large German church!)* It tells people, "Your kids were not important enough for us to prepare in advance."

Greeters – Our experience in visiting churches often started with two or three people who met us at the door, offered a fake smile and a handshake, and then acted as if to say, "Now move along. Go enjoy the service. Leave us alone so we can do our job. Ba-bye!" This reeks of inauthenticity, something Millennials can spot from a mile away and want to avoid like the plague.

At our church we chose only *genuinely* friendly, happy and enthusiastic people for our greeter team. We had greeters stationed at the front door and as they walked into the adult service room. We reminded our Team that EVERYONE is a greeter as long as people are around. We encouraged them to "read" the visitor's body language and engage them in conversation if they were open. If not, our people were expected to simply offer a smile, a handshake and a welcoming greeting. This was because many Germans don't like making small talk with someone they've never met before.

Greeters are the face of your ministry. They, along with the parking lot attendants, are the first contact many people have with your church. You can't afford to have a moody, shy or self-involved person serve in this area. Your greeters set the mood for the visitor's entire experience! This is why Disney spends *up to eight full weeks* training their parking lot attendants![73]

Welcoming atmosphere – This has to flow from the top down. General observation reveals that a church takes on the personality of its pastor. If the pastor goes out of his/her way to notice visitors and to make everyone feel genuinely welcome, his/her people will do the same. These things need to be taught and modeled. Pastors need to love their sheep *and their visitors* enough to go out of their way to connect with them, and to only hire people who share this heart.

Post-service – It is just as important – maybe even *more so* – to be welcoming *after* the service! It is at this time that visitors determine whether or not you have credibility. They may still be deciding whether or not to come back; and this is the make or break point!

In many of the churches we visited some people were quite friendly before the service, but after the service they talked with their friends and ignored us. Even worse, they stood in the walkways or doorways with their coffee to the point that we had to ask them to move out of the way so we could leave. Even though we were *obviously* visitors (we were walking around with the first time visitor packet they gave us when we walked in) we felt invisible. There was no one looking for visitors so they could help them find the Visitor Info Booth or to offer them a cup of coffee and engage them in conversation.

Your Info Booth needs to be the most welcoming environment in the entire church. Common sense would say that you need friendly people serving there who live and breathe your church's culture and know the organization. But they also need to try to connect the visitor to someone who can help them find the Kids Church, get a cup of coffee or find a seat. In our church we had a lady serving in our Info Booth that seemed to have a supernatural gift in that area. Return visitors would come over to talk with her, get prayer or just a warm hug.

Never forget that the service isn't over for people until they drive away, so train your people to be welcoming after the service as well. One of our mantras was, *"**Everything** is part of the message, from the moment they arrive to the moment they leave."* The sermon didn't just start when I stepped up to share the message. It started the moment they arrived. Everything we do communicates something to a visitor. They are asking,

"Can I trust what they are telling me? Do they *really believe* what they are saying? Are they smoking what they're selling?"

We have to be intentional about connecting with visitors. The natural human tendency is to form a closed circle of relationships. We can't afford this in our churches. If God sends us unchurched people we need to value them as much as He does.

The Less-Than-Desirables

In two of the churches we served, God brought unchurched teens (gangster wannabes) into our youth group. Of course we welcomed them and treated them like part of the family, which led to many of these students committing their lives to Christ. But this caused a problem with some parents of our "church" kids. These parents didn't want their kids in that "threatening environment" with "those sort of kids."

I explained that we shouldn't expect unchurched people to act like people who have grown up in church. After you've been in church for a while you learn all the do's and don'ts. But people coming in fresh off the street have no clue. We can't hold them to the same standard that is difficult for even our regular attenders to achieve. But we can position our staff/volunteers so that everyone is kept safe.

If God answers our prayers and the unchurched do visit our churches, they will bring all their issues with them. Their lives will be messy. They won't know how they are supposed to dress, talk or behave in church. Unfortunately people that have been in church for a while quickly learn how to talk and act – and how to hide their issues, because everyone knows that "holy" people don't struggle with difficult issues (note my sarcasm). This pharisaical behavior modification helps no one.

We have to be welcoming to people with messy lives (just like ours!) and remember that the goal isn't compliance; it's accepting people just as they are. Isn't this exactly how God accepted us? Paul put it this way: "While we were still sinners, Christ died for us."[74] This mindset has to come from the top down. When our people see their pastors and leaders bringing the unchurched to the services and *truly* welcoming those that visit, they will follow our lead.

Many churches truly do want unchurched people in their churches. Unfortunately, they all-to-often only want unchurched people that look like them. We've worked with far too many churches that say they want the unchurched to come, but when people that are economically challenged, from different racial or cultural backgrounds or from the LBGT community show up, they all but close the doors. We worked with a church that had an entire team meeting on how to deal with the gay couple that attended the previous Sunday. They asked how we should respond to gays, to which I replied, "I just give them a big hug and say, 'Welcome to church! I'm glad you're here!'" I would much rather have someone from the LGBT community in our services hearing about a God that loves them and wants to get involved in his/her life than out on the street believing that God hates them. This wasn't an acceptable answer in their eyes. They would much rather that the pastor immediately launch into a sermon series on sin.

If we ever want to see the unchurched become a part of our faith communities we'll have to be to be more accepting and less critical. The only people Jesus had very pointed words for were the hypocritical religious leaders of His day. They felt they had this whole "God thing" figured out. They knew much better than those around them how to please God and earn His favor. But their self-righteous attitude earned Jesus' rebuke instead.

We also have to be open to interruptions. Opportunities often come dressed as problems and inconveniences. Although I usually take advantage of these, I missed two major God-given opportunities in Freiburg because they would have been extremely inconvenient.

One was when a homeless guy showed up for our church service. He actually never came inside the building, but waited outside to talk with me after the service. My team engaged him in conversation, but he said he really wanted to talk with me. As we talked I felt the Holy Spirit nudging me to take him out to lunch. I was exhausted after an extremely long weekend. My family was tired, too, and just wanted to go home (we only had one car), so I gave him some cash and went home with them instead of obeying God's leading.

Another time I was waiting on the last train of the night that would take me home from Freiburg (we lived 45 minutes away) at the end of a very long day. I was at the train station McDonald's drinking a cup of coffee and using the free Wi-Fi. I noticed a teen across the restaurant from me was playing with his mobile phone. As my departure time grew near I realized God wanted me to talk with this guy. I knew what I should do, but I was exhausted, with no place in town to stay for the night, and I just wanted to get home to my family. I ended up leaving and hopping on my train.

To this day the memory of these lost opportunities haunts me. I *never* want to miss another one!

Connecting With Visitors

Here's the conundrum pastors face: if you don't get visitors into your church, and then retain them, it will die. Every year people move away, start attending other churches or quit attending church altogether. Most churches have an annual attrition rate of 20%. We want to avoid this, but it's inevitable. In order to offset this loss we need a steady stream of visitors. And we need to retain a healthy percentage of them. We really have to keep our eye on the ball in this area!

On the other hand, if you don't minister to your regular attenders they will vote with their feet (by leaving). You have to do both at the same time. We discovered a way to simultaneously accomplish both. We incorporated bringing visitors them into our discipleship strategy. It became a part of our spiritual formation process.

Through teaching, training and modeling we taught our members to be welcoming to visitors. This was so that they would value visitors enough to get out of their comfort zone and actually "be the Church." This must become a part of your church culture, which flows from the pastor's heart and actions. Our team modeled this; and we reminded our church often that *they* were as much a part of the hospitality team as those with badges on.

Many churches have "greeters" – team members at the door whose job is to welcome people as they enter. After the service is over, the visitors are often directed to go back to a special room where they can meet the pastors. We ditched this model in favor of a more organic one. While we did have greeters at the door, we stressed that every person – even the "newbies" – should join us in welcoming our visitors. We encouraged everyone to invite a visitor to sit with them and to join him or her for a cup of coffee before, and again after, the service, and also to introduce the visitor to others. Such relationships are what make our churches "sticky."

We trained our leaders and workers to identify people they hadn't seen before. When they identified a visitor they were to introduce themselves and engage the person in conversation, if possible. They then brought them to the Info Table where the visitor was given a small gift (a travel mug or shopping bag). When our people saw a person with a visitor gift in hand they could then engage them as a first or second time visitor. This made it easier when encouraging our church to be welcoming to visitors.

We even instructed our volunteers to stop whatever they were doing, if necessary, if it gave them the opportunity to engage the visitors in conversation. This was very counter-cultural in task-driven Germany! It is also one of the reasons we created teams to serve in every area of ministry. If one person stopped serving coffee or cleaning to talk with a visitor, someone else could pick up the slack. And if the task didn't get done until after the service, so be it.

Even since returning to the US we've seen churches blow big opportunities to really connect with visitors by engaging with them after the service. Most churches work so hard on making their first impression a good one. But as we said, we taught our team that EVERYTHING we do and EVERYONE they meet – from the moment they drive into the parking lot until they drive away – is a part of the sermon. What happens before the sermon shows a visitor whether or not a church is worth their time. But it's what happens after the service is over that reveals whether or not we really believe what we say.

Genuine Acceptance

What does it look like to truly accept someone? In the Bible we find that Jesus embodied this concept:

- His conversation with a Samaritan woman – She had been used and discarded by several men, and was now living with another man. Any self-respecting first century Rabbi wouldn't even venture into Samaria, much less speak with a *woman* – especially one who had such a tainted reputation. He spoke to the hunger in her soul for spiritual truth.[75]

- The woman caught in the act of adultery – The Pharisees interrupted Jesus' impromptu teaching session by dragging this woman before Him, demanding that she be stoned to death. Jesus defended her by confronting their hypocrisy.[76]

- Zacchaeus – Here was a man who took advantage of His fellow Jews by collecting taxes for Rome. Tax collectors were a hated bunch, being considered traitors. But Jesus connected with outsiders by having dinner at Zacchaeus' house.[77]

- Peter – As he waited on the outcome of Jesus' trial, he denied knowing Jesus three times. After His resurrection Jesus offered Peter forgiveness and restored him to his place of leadership among the disciples.[78]

Notice that Jesus seemed to prefer the company of "imperfect people" to that of those that pretended to have it all together. Dr. Gerald Brooks says you need to decide if you will pastor imperfect people. If you have to have only perfect people in your church, it will remain small and will never reach outsiders.

Our churches are already full of imperfect people – people just like us! If we choose to be authentic and vulnerable our people will be as well, and they will feel safe enough to reach out and get the help they so desperately need. If we instead choose to act as if we are perfect Christian role models (whatever *that* looks like), our people will be as *fake* as we are and continue to suffer alone in silence.

Tolerance

As we said in the first section of this book, tolerance is an important topic in Western society. While it is important to be tolerant of other ideologies and worldviews, we can't forget the North Star (indicator of true north) presented in Scripture. Although it's not a popular subject, absolute truth is a reality, and not just a subjective issue. There are certain biblical standards that believers are instructed to live by. But we need to act with grace, not judgment toward those that are struggling. And we can never afford to judge *outsiders* by *insider* standards.[79]

The Church is famous for defining itself by its "enemies," being known by what it stands against rather than what it stands for. Its reputation is one of judgment and hypocrisy. People that don't fit the church mold have been shamed, shunned or ignored until they go away. WE HAVE TO CHANGE THIS PERCEPTION!

How accepting are you of someone that is wildly different than you? What about your church? You may think that your church is more enlightened than most. Just try bringing someone to visit that is "inappropriately dressed" and see how people look at him or her. It's tough to overcome our entrenched ideas and habits.

A pastor friend in Bonn, Germany was telling me of a time he was baptizing a new believer that had absolutely no church background whatsoever. As is their church's custom in baptisms, the pastor asked the man to give a quick version of his conversion story. While telling his story the man dropped a few major curse words, which shocked the crowd a bit. But this church is so excited about people coming to Christ that they cheered wildly when he was baptized.

Would your church do that? This pastor had both communicated and modeled God's heart toward the people that are the farthest from Him, and his church got the message loud and clear! Pastors, we must make this change in *our* hearts if we want our churches to impact the world around us and connect with the unchurched.

The "Norm"

There are certain expectations in the church world of what a Christian should look, smell, dress and act like – the "Norm." These are all based on external criteria. These types of expectations are based on rules that don't really work to restrain the natural desires of our selfish nature.[80] Actually Jesus called people that judged others based on outward appearance "hypocrites," a Greek word meaning, "play actors."

In our inaugural service we had a drug-addicted, alcoholic prostitute give her heart to Christ. Shortly thereafter we had a homosexual couple come a few times. One of the lesbians had radically different political and cultural views than we did. But because we valued her as a person more than we valued our opinion she said she felt at home with us. While we didn't condone her lifestyle, every time she came she heard a very clear message of salvation. That wouldn't have happened had we confronted her about her lifestyle choices from the beginning. *(For the record, at our church we had* **vastly** *different expectations of* attenders *than we did of* leaders.)

We also had a few Muslim families that attend our services on a semi-regular basis. Robin prayed with a Muslim lady to commit her life to Jesus after a service. She told Robin afterward, "Now I can pray to Jesus, Allah and Buddha." Rather than freaking out and correcting her, we just encouraged her to keep coming back. She didn't know any better. What she needed was grace, not rebuke. Every week she came she heard more about Jesus. Because of how we welcomed her family, her Muslim-raised kids committed their hearts to Christ and have only missed a handful of services since. Even her husband committed his life to Christ. Because they continued to come, we were able to get them started on the discipleship pathway. And they continued to actively bring their friends!

Chapter 12
Entry Level Ministry

All pastors know that they need to get their people involved in serving if they want to increase the amount and quality of ministry they are able to offer. If not, they'd better have a huge budget so they can hire a lot of people. We need to make it easy for people to get involved on a serving team. This is the best way to help our people to use their gifts to make a genuine impact in lives.

A Large Shallow End

Growing up in church we were trained to always "guard the pulpit." This meant that we were not to let anyone into a position of ministry until they were *thoroughly* trained and exhibited the lifestyle of a *true* disciple of Christ. I do understand the logic behind this. Paul wrote that we shouldn't place novices into positions of leadership. It would prove detrimental to them and those they lead.

But too many churches feel that this also applies to serving positions. A person isn't allowed to serve in any capacity until they truly buy into the vision and mission of the church, having gone through the entire membership and discipleship process. I can understand this in high-responsibility or high-trust areas such as kids ministry or handling the offering. But should it be a necessary prerequisite in order for someone to serve coffee, help with setup or work with the media team? Shouldn't they be able to serve *while* they are going through the process?

I wonder if we are going about the discipleship process backward. Are we inadvertently crippling a person's ability to experience biblical discipleship in our efforts to guard the "purity" of ministry in our churches? Doesn't it produce a feeling of ownership when we develop clear and easy pathways for participation? In language training this is called "learning by immersion," and it is by far the most effective form of learning.

We need to remove any unnecessary obstacles that keep people from serving. We just have to determine what the definition of "unnecessary" is for our context. I heard a pastor put it this way, "We used to think that once people are discipled we need to get them to serve. Today we get people to serve in order for them to experience discipleship."

I think this is a key to discipling the coming generations. They want action, not mere words. They learn best by hands-on training. We simply need to help them process what they're experiencing, turning every event into a teaching opportunity. This means we must develop more coaches, which enables seasoned leaders to bring their wisdom and insight to bear in facilitating the development of younger disciples/leaders.

Some of the best advice I received during my church planter training with ARC (Association of Related Churches) was, "Create a large shallow end of the pool." In a swimming pool the shallow end is for beginners and the deep end is for more advanced swimmers. Anyone can do just fine in the shallow end, even small children (though they may need to be watched).

Good swimmers do what people in the deep end of the pool do: they dive, they do flips, and yes, they swim. It's easy to tell that they are deep-enders. But people in the shallow end need to get familiar with the water. They need to learn how to hold their breath underwater, how to open their eyes underwater... and how to swim. They will probably start by "dog paddling." This requires no skill; just a strong desire not to drown!

These "dog paddle" ministries should be low-risk activities such as setting up or tearing down (for mobile churches), grilling at a BBQ, serving in the media team, serving coffee or helping the ushers or the greeting team by assisting the elderly or holding umbrellas for people arriving on rainy days. Outreach and service projects should be open to everyone.

We can't afford to offer only deep end serving positions, or require deep end-type commitment levels. We have to create dog paddle opportunities for people to get involved. This must be done intentionally. It doesn't happen by accident. God has given all of us gifts and talents, experiences and passions that are to be used for the furtherance of His Kingdom. The Gospel has always spread more rapidly when people are encouraged to just "get out there and serve." They don't need 36 hours of training; they just need to use their gifts.

If every person in a serving position has to be *vetted* we won't have nearly as many people in the game. And the people that do get involved will often be overworked. Furthermore, as an associate pastor I saw that the pastoral staff/area leaders often ended up "fighting" over the people that *were* vetted in order to fill holes in their section of the organizational chart. But if *everyone* is allowed to serve this pressure is greatly reduced and more people take ownership in the church and its vision.

Layne Schwanz from Church of the Highlands in Birmingham, AL says their goal is to get as many people as possible involved in small groups. In order for this to happen they need a large number of small group hosts and leaders. They do give a basic training session for their leaders and hosts, but most of the training is done "on the job" – as they serve. Their premise is that most small group leader training prepares people for situations they will never face. The small group leaders and hosts regularly meet with "coaches" that walk them through the steps of leading/hosting a group and answer any questions they have. This enables them to get more people involved, and to more efficiently move people from the shallow end into the deep end of the pool.

Only Perfect People Need Apply
When planting Watermark God spoke *very clearly* to us to create places for people to use their gifts, even if they weren't fully serving Him. God *clearly* directed us to allow musicians/singers that weren't "model Christ-followers" to use

their gifts to help people worship. Our purpose was supposed to drive our practice. As we'll discuss more in the chapters on Alignment, pastors should always evaluate their programs, strategy and hiring through the lens of their vision and values.

This was such a HUGE shock to me! I had always been taught that if a person wasn't fully serving God they weren't prepared to be a part of the worship team, much less be onstage *at all*. The interesting thing about this was that our standard of measurement only examined external factors (things people do/don't do) as spiritual qualifications. I was trained that putting such people on the worship team would "dilute the anointing" on the worship. We might as well have put a disclaimer on the worship team application: "*Only perfect people need apply.*"

But now it was very clear to us that we needed to bring in people that were NOT serving God, as long as they would be committed. Of course we had some basic requirements, but on the worship team we made it as easy as possible for people with musical gifts to get involved. As a matter of fact, we had a drummer for a couple of months that would come with a hangover from time to time. This was a frustration to us, but we knew what God had told us. He wasn't the best drummer, but was okay. He was the best we had at the time. One of the band members tried to disciple him, but the man ended up leaving.

After this guy left, this same band member asked for permission to invite his friend to play drums for us, even though this guy wasn't serving God. His friend was a truly gifted musician. He could play any instrument on the stage better than the rest of us. But his life was a mess. He came and visited a service, and I talked with him afterward.

He said he loved the "no pressure" approach we took with people and the no-hype, down-to-earth service style. He had helped plant a few churches many years before and had been burned by a couple of them. I sensed more than anything else that as an artist he hadn't measured up to their standard of how a Christian should look and act. Artists are simply wired differently than the rest of the population.

I asked if he would be willing to play drums for our church. His response was, "You know I'm not serving God, right? My life and my marriage are a mess." I said, "No problem. If you would commit to play with us on a weekly basis we will work through the problems. We are more concerned with what goes on in a person's heart than how perfect he appears." He agreed to play with us.

A month later he came to me in tears after the service. He said that he had given his life back to Jesus and committed to fully follow Him. Over the course of the next three years we watched his life change. Today his family is thriving and he is taking steps towards the ministry dream that he had given up on. This would have never happened had we demanded that only "perfect" people get to serve.

We did everything we could to get people into serving positions. And because we made serving a part of our church culture we didn't have much of a problem getting people involved. We accepted people where they were and helped them find a place where they could use their gifts.

Our main training tool was also a part of our discipleship process. A new person "shadowed" a more experienced team member – watching, then working alongside them. In German culture this is a normal part of the job training process so it worked very well for us. The most important thing in this process is that the experienced team member carries the DNA of the church. This is critical because spiritual DNA is more *caught* than *taught*.

This "mentor" should not only show him or her the ropes, but also help him or her understand the vision and why this serving ministry is so important. Because of this, the mentor needs to know how to cast vision. It can be something as simple as, "Every chair I setup provides a seat for someone to connect with God and get their life right with Him. This will impact not only their life, but all the lives within their circle of influence. I pray over each chair as I set it up and ask God to speak clearly to the person that sits in it."

The mentor is also responsible for helping connect the mentee with others in leadership, in their serving team and in the church. It is a good low-pressure way to help people get involved in the life of the church.

Specialized Skill Set Required

Andy Stanley encourages pastors to identify and tap into the skills of successful businesspeople in their churches. Many pastors – me included – don't have any gifting in the area of finances and business. Thank God Robin has some business experience! But why should we try to reinvent the wheel? We should leverage the natural gifts God gives people and allow them to use their gifts for the glory of God. They are already using their gifts successfully in the business world. Why not use them to build God's Kingdom? *We'll talk more about this in the chapters on Alignment.*

People with highly specific skill sets can be brought together into a team to work on a project basis, such as the cost analysis of an upcoming event or outreach, creating a video, a print or social media campaign, website design or facility management and improvement. These allow a high capacity person to use their gifts for a significant purpose without making a long-term commitment, and they allow you to use volunteers (as opposed to contract labor) to expand the church and its reach. And it whets the volunteer's appetite for serving on a longer-term basis.

I need to add the caveat that we never allowed someone that knowingly led an *openly* anti-biblical lifestyle to be in *leadership*. Leading and serving are two very different things. Being in leadership is taking on a recognized position of influence. There is a huge responsibility that comes with spiritual leadership. If I move someone into leadership simply because they are gifted I risk damaging both their spiritual growth process, and that of those they influence. This is definitely an area where we as leaders need to be led by the Holy Spirit.

Chapter 13
Preaching The Gospel In A Post-Christian Context

Because of the biblical backdrop that was a part of American culture up until Generation X, the emphasis in sermons was on content. Every message needed to have three points and a poem. Today's younger generations are for the most part biblically illiterate, so the focus needs to be on the application of that content. Back in the day there was a basic trust of churches and a respect for pastors. This is no longer the case, so we need to start from scratch.

Millennials are used to 3 - 5 minute TV scenes, 140 character tweets, short YouTube video clips and media soundbites. They are over-stimulated and easily bored. If you want to reach them you have to get to the point. If you ramble you will lose them. The days of the effectiveness of long sermons have come and gone. We always want to leave our audience wanting more rather than wanting less.

Remember, the goal of our messages needs to be the life application and transformation of our hearers, not just the transfer of information. We've found it's better to take one or two seeds and plant them deep in the hearts of our hearers than to scatter a bunch of seeds on top of the ground and hope for the best. What's more useful: to take one or two points and really drive them home or to give a bunch of points and hope your people remember something? The latter has been referred to as the spaghetti method of preaching, which references an interesting method of testing to see if the spaghetti is ready: throw a bunch of it against the wall and see if something sticks.

Church In A Vacuum

When I was young churches could make the basic assumption that people knew – or at least were familiar with – the Bible. Most people could quote at least part of John 3:16 and Psalm 23. The Bible was a part of the fabric of American society. That's not the case anymore.

In other words, we need to learn to do church in a vacuum. A vacuum is empty. It contains nothing. We need to design our church services – especially our messages – as if they existed in a vacuum because, in a sense, they do. The unchurched bring no biblical experience with them. We can't expect people to understand what we are talking about when we mention Bible characters or stories.

At the same time, we can't assume a teacher/pupil stance. We need to approach our teaching and conversations from a relational, peer-to-peer perspective. To act as if we have all the answers not only seems arrogant, it causes people to shut down. We can never learn where people are coming from if we won't listen – *really listen* – to them and get to know their stories. This helps us connect with their hearts.

Because the next generations are so relativistic and pluralistic we have to learn how to share the truth of the Gospel without being dogmatic. It is counterproductive to read a Bible verse and say something to the effect of: "That's what the Bible says. It's the truth. Take it or leave it."

As we taught, Robin and I learned to share differing viewpoints, but to always bring the topic back to the Bible. This worked well for us in a couple of ways. First, it highlights the fact that we realize there are other viewpoints than ours. We don't come off as condescending or combative. Instead we show that we are open to conversation. This creates a safe place for people that believe differently than us. It was this very attitude that attracted two Muslim families to our church. They continued to attend because, as one mother told us, "When we come here we get hope and feel peace." One entire Muslim family ended up committing their lives to Christ.

Secondly, if our people can't learn to process opposing worldviews in light of the Bible message they will be easy prey in a world that is hostile to Christianity. It will eat them alive! We have to teach our people how to interpret current events, pop culture and other worldviews through the lens of biblical truth. Biblical truth is just as relevant today as it was in Jesus' day.

Consider Your Audience

The first rule of communication is to know your audience. WHO you are speaking to will determine HOW you should present the message on your heart. You would normally communicate with a three-year-old differently than you would with a college student. It should be the same way with your messages. A sermon for a youth group should be different than one written for a geriatric audience.

Pastor Rick Warren of Saddleback Church in Lake Forest, CA asserts in *The Purpose Driven Church*, "The crowd does not determine whether or not you speak the truth: The truth is not optional. But your audience does determine which truths you choose to speak about. And some truths are more relevant than others to unbelievers. Can something be both true and irrelevant? Certainly!" The Bible says 'Speak *only* what is helpful for building others up *according to their needs*, that it may benefit those who listen.'[81] *[emphasis mine]* This is not a shallow marketing tip. God commands it!

As our society becomes more and more unchurched we will need to adjust our language and communication style if we want to reach them. Only in churches do you hear words like salvation, redemption, sanctification and sin, and phrases like "Who you are in Christ" or "Born Again." Of course these are Bible words and phrases, but we need to realize that our hearers may not understand what they mean. Such terms may even carry negative connotations with the unchurched – especially in a Post-Christian context.

One of the most confusing and uncomfortable things that unchurched people experience when visiting a church is the use of "Christianese" – words like, "Hallelujah, glory, praise the

Lord, and amen." These are simply Christian filler words that really don't mean anything to the person saying or hearing it! We've become so accustomed to saying them in a Christian setting that we often don't even realize we're saying them. I realize this statement may offend some people. But if you will connect with unchurched young adults in THEIR world you'll see that they NEVER use these words, except to make fun of religious people. And I *beg* you to LOSE the "preacher voice!" If you wanted to build a crowd in the 50s, 60s and 70s you needed it, but it just doesn't work today.

With this in mind we need to prepare and communicate our messages in a way that unchurched people and visitors can connect with. Pastors often make the mistake of preaching to those in the room rather than to those that haven't yet come through their doors. If your messages are not focused on connecting with 18 - 25 year olds you won't have to worry about how to connect with an unchurched audience. *If* they come they probably won't stay.

Let me say that again, if we are unwilling to grow in our communication skills – especially those skills that connect with an unchurched audience – we probably won't see many opportunities to reach people that are far from God. We don't need to change *what* we say, but rather *how* we say it.

The Amen Corner

> *"I would sooner bring one sinner to Jesus Christ than unravel all the mysteries of the divine Word, for salvation is the one thing we are to live for."*[82]

Charles Spurgeon

Robin and I quickly learned that the people God wanted us to reach weren't the ones that were "amenning" our sermons. They were just sitting there, taking it all in, trying to determine if we were the real deal and attempting to process what our message meant to their lives. If you *have* to have a response – "Can I get an amen?" – you won't be very effective with the unchurched.

If we're not careful, we'll end up preaching to the "Amen Corner" because they are the ones that give us positive feedback. Unfortunately, the Amen Corner usually only amens you when you preach theologically and spiritually "deep" messages, things that *they* like to hear. But these types of messages rarely come with practical "meat and potatoes" application. Besides, what's *deeper* than loving God and loving your neighbor?

If you'll study Jesus' style of preaching/teaching, you'll see that a large percentage of it was highly practical. In contrast, the Amen Corner wants preaching that makes them feel as if they've learned a deep spiritual truth, but doesn't really require very much of them. Our goal as pastors should be to train our people to feed themselves spiritually and be actively involved in discipleship and the disciple-making process.

Cultural Bridges

The Apostle Paul, author of a large part of the New Testament, communicated to people with language, expressions and metaphors that were familiar to them. He apparently was a sports fan because he used a number of sports metaphors. He compares competing in the Olympic Games with fulfilling our God-given destiny[83] and living out our faith with boxing and running.[84] He even likens ministry to military service.[85]

In Acts 17 Luke, Paul's biographer, writes that when speaking to Jews he quoted from their Scriptures but when dealing with Greek philosophers he used a mystical pagan altar to point to Christ. He even used pagan poetry to convey his message.[86] He was a master at finding cultural bridges to the Gospel.

So was Jesus. He used cultural icons[87], political figures[88] and even current events.[89] He was the oldest son of a carpenter, and would have been trained to assist his natural father, Joseph. But how many carpentry illustrations did He use in His teaching? NONE! His audience consisted primarily of fishermen, shepherds and farmers so He spoke of fish, nets, seeds, trees, flowers and sheep. It was the world His hearers knew.

If we're going to effectively share the life-giving message of God's grace, we need to adapt it to our hearers. As I mentioned before, any good missionary will take time to study the local culture – the language and customs, hopes and fears, dreams and desires, struggles and concerns – to find connection points. When we first moved to Germany God made something clear to me on the airplane somewhere over the Atlantic Ocean. His voice was unmistakable and full of authority! He said, "Don't you DARE expect them [the people to whom we were sent] to speak *your* heart language to come to Me!" So after we settled in one the first things we did was to start studying the local language and culture. Even today when our family speaks German it is not the *Hochdeutsch* (High German) taught in school. We speak German with the *Kölsch* accent that is common on the streets of Bonn and Cologne.

You can learn about the language and society in class or on the Internet, but there is no substitute for actual cultural immersion. You can study it for years but unless you place yourself in the actual setting you will miss some important things. We *must* become students of the culture around us. The best way to do this is to immerse ourselves in the lives of those we're called to reach.

The Bible *DOES* Matter

The younger generations just aren't interested in the Bible anymore. Sadly, there is a lot of data to support this assertion. As a matter of fact, at the time of this writing the Barna organization just published the results from a survey of Millenials' feelings about the Bible.

Among non-Christian young adults:

- 45% believe the Bible to be a book of teachings written by men that contains stories and advice.

- 30% believe the Bible is merely a useful book of moral teachings.

- 19% believe it is an outdated book with no relevance for today.

- 27% believe it is a dangerous book of religious dogma used for centuries to oppress people.

The good news is that 96% of young believers maintain that it is the actual or inspired Word of God. And many of them are reading it on a regular basis.[90]

Studies like these reveal the overall direction and opinion of younger generations. But we have found that if you give an unchurched person a *reason* to read/hear Scripture they will engage. Gone are the days where we can simply quote a Scripture and expect them to give us their attention. Unfortunately, many of them see the Bible as merely a book of wise sayings. As we grew up preachers would start off their sermons by saying, "Turn in your Bibles," and everyone just did it. Today's younger generations usually don't even own a Bible; or if they do, they only have a digital version on their smartphone or tablet.

We have to show them *why* Scripture is important to them and *how* it applies to their lives. It's not enough to just throw out the information and expect them to connect the dots. We have to spell it out for them. They are not dumb by any means. Actually, most young adults are highly educated, and we need to speak to that. But we do need to make biblical principles and doctrine accessible to "everyman." To communicate like this takes more effort, especially if our normal speaking style is different than this. But the results are worth it!

Whatever you do, don't speak down to them. They are NOT dumb! Not knowing the Bible doesn't mean someone is dumb any more than not knowing about quantum physics means someone is an idiot. Actually many of your unchurched visitors will probably be quite intelligent. Speak to that. Because our church had many university students, in our sermons we commended their desire for knowledge and wisdom.

Andy Vom Steeg, pastor of New Vintage Church in Santa Rosa, CA, explains, "A lot of the people who come to our church have no church background at all. They don't know the stories of faith, so I can't just allude to Noah or Abraham or the feeding of the five thousand and expect them to understand. I have to tell people to pick up a Bible and turn to the table of contents to find the passage for that message."[91]

Our problem comes when we try to impress the unchurched with our biblical knowledge. This is wasted effort. They are very pragmatic. If a Bible principle actually works in the real world, they're all ears. By observing Andy Stanley I learned the importance of intentionally speaking to the unchurched ("newbies") and addressing their fears. It's okay to let unchurched visitors know that the point you're trying to make applies more to believers. But be sure to remind them not to check out so they can catch the parts of your message that apply to them as well.

Make It Plain

The days of theoretical preaching are over. Many of the preachers I grew up hearing should have taught in the seminaries where they studied. There was a lot of information, but not much in the way of application. They just expected people to connect the dots on their own.

We need to be very practical in our teaching. It's imperative that we give them something that connects Sunday with Monday. We pastors usually get to rest on Monday while most of our people head out into the fray. We need to give them practical ways to start applying the message on Monday morning. By doing so we are teaching them how to glean practical principles out of Scripture for themselves.

I love what Rick Warren says, "Your messages need to answer two questions: 'So What?' and 'Now What?'" We need to make sure they know why this message is important to them and where to go from here. We need to give them "next steps" that they can start doing either today at home or tomorrow at work/school. If you look at Jesus' teaching as recorded by His biographers, He was very strong on practical application. We must teach the same way!

We need to clearly define the decision(s) we want them to make. Our listeners need to know the step we're asking them to take. The structure and content of our messages should move them toward that decision. And we need to help them see what this decision looks like in the real world.

Take Home Points

According to the Barna Group, when asked to think about their last church visit, three out of five church attenders said they could not remember a significant or important new insight or understanding related to faith.[92] We can't afford to waste a single opportunity to plant life-giving truths from the Word of God deep into the hearts of our people!

I've heard some great communicators say, "If you are only going to remember one thing from my message today, I want it to be this…" It helps their hearers to know what they consider most important. If not overused, it is a great way to make sure they are still engaged.

Jeff Henderson, Lead Pastor of Gwinnett Church calls these "Tweetable moments." He often asks, "What 140 character statements do you want your people to take home with them?" It will give them an answer to the question, "What did your pastor teach on last Sunday?"

You should always look for ways to connect your message to your mission, vision and values. What gets rewarded (by placing emphasis on it) gets repeated (in practice). If you can tie your message points – especially your take home points – into your mission, vision and values, even the visitors will begin to see who God has called your church to be.

Hope

Napoleon Bonaparte famously said, "A leader is a dealer in hope." This is especially true of pastors! The world around us seems to suck the life right out of people. Your audience deals with growing living expenses and crushing debt, greater demands and longer hours on the job, ever-increasing relational stress and the constant drone of negativity in the news. Our churches need to be places of refuge where people can get a hope recharge. Our messages must carry the reminder that because Jesus is alive there is hope. We are called to impart life to people.

The invitation

We always want to give people a chance to respond to the message they've just heard. Whether we label it an altar call, a response time or an invitation doesn't matter. We've learned not to assume that everyone in the room has a vibrant relationship with Jesus Christ, so we want to give people a chance to make a commitment to God in one way or another. Some churches have people making a commitment to Christ come down front. Others have the people close their eyes, bow their heads and raise their hands. The important thing is to at least provide them with the opportunity to do so.

At the end of my first message to our youth group in Texas I invited the teens to commit their lives to Christ. One of the girls from the worship team raised her hand. One of our leaders took her to the prayer room and asked her why she raised her hand. She said she needed to give her heart to Jesus. When she was asked why she had never done so before, she replied, "No one has ever asked me if I wanted to." This was a young lady that had been involved in this youth group for a while. Every week the former youth pastor had given the same type of invitation, but for whatever reason, this time it connected with her heart. What if I didn't ask on this night? I would have missed a God-given opportunity.

I know many pastors that just go through the same memorized invitation routine at the end of their messages. It sounds as if it is memorized. The pastor might as well be a telemarketer reading from a cue card. This is NOT okay! We are inviting people to step from death into life, to move from the kingdom of darkness into the kingdom of light, to enter into a relationship with the God of the universe. It is a BIG DEAL!

We need to connect the invitation to the message as much as possible. This continues the flow of the service and keeps people engaged. Our messages should point to Christ, so the logical next step of inviting people to commit their lives to Him shouldn't be difficult to make. We need to look for creative ways to make this invitation both fresh and powerful. If the message or the service doesn't lend itself to giving an invitation, at least make that available to the people: "There will be some staff and altar care workers down at the front of the stage after the service. If you have questions about what it means to follow Christ or need prayer, they are here for you."

Discussion Questions:

Name some traditions or customs churches have that create unnecessary barriers for the unchurched? What about in YOUR church... can you identify any?

What does a visitor see when they walk into your church?

What tweaks can you make to increase your church's welcome factor?

Do you agree or disagree with the shallow end ministry *analogy? Why or why not? If so, what shallow end ministries exist at your church? What shallow end ministry opportunities can you create in your setting?*

What tweaks do you need to make in your communication style in order to make the Gospel more accessible to an unchurched person?

ALIGNMENT

Empowering The People God Sends You

Leadership development is probably the most underestimated and misunderstood area of church ministry, so I will spend a considerable amount of time on this topic. Most churches are exceptional at attracting warm bodies and plugging them into holes in their organizational charts. Churches that actually empower their people and release them to do real ministry are few and far between. For far too long ministry has been left up to the "professionals" (ministers) because they are "called" and trained. *We have to change this mindset!* It's neither biblical nor beneficial. Actually it is *toxic*, both to churches and their pastors.

Pastors, along with other spiritual leaders, are called to equip believers so that THEY can do the work of the ministry.[93] Pastors are expected to get their people out of the stands and onto the field. In order to do this we must empower our people to lead, giving them actual leadership responsibilities and authority. They will surprise us with their creativity and passion. God has created them to do the work of the ministry. Pastors need to train them, release them to minister and then get out of their way!

Chapter 14
Leading Younger Generations

Leadership isn't for the faint of heart. If you want to lead it will cost you dearly. You will have to give up your time, your emotional and spiritual energy, your resources and your rights in order to lead others. It will be the most painful, yet rewarding, thing you've ever done. No one you lead will be able to understand the sacrifices you have to make. But neither will anyone else sense the pleasure of God like you do when you move a group of people toward God's dream for their lives.

The image of leadership that is trumpeted by our culture is based on calculated networking and cutthroat ladder climbing. It is all about gaining prestige, power and privilege. Unfortunately the unchurched leaders God sends us will bring this mindset with them. We will have to combat this mindset by modeling, teaching and coaching.

Leading as Jesus did is the polar opposite of this "me-first" mindset. God-honoring leadership is selfless. It requires us to "lay down your life"[94] – our dreams, our desires and our preferences – for the people we are called to lead. We have to work harder and give more than everyone else in the organization. In the most basic analysis, leaders are the greatest servants of all.

Thankfully we have been privileged to learn from some amazing leaders. My pastor travels around the USA training leaders from churches of all sizes. He taught us to process everything through the filter of leadership, to look through leadership glasses. We have been trained to seek out leaders, empower them and let them lead. This was the secret to the momentum and rapid growth we experienced at Watermark.

Cultural Expectations

Millennials see the leadership process very different than Baby Boomers do. With Boomers, organizational leadership development was linear and orderly. The rungs on the corporate ladder were clearly defined. It was assumed that patience and hard work were required to get to the top. There was an understanding of authority systems and a basic trust for the system. In most churches the Bible was the final authority. But this began to change with Gen X and the transition to postmodernism.

With Millennials and every following generation the landscape will be drastically different. People no longer trust the system. They no longer look to "authority figures" for the answers. Why would you do that when you could easily Google any question you have?

One of the most striking differences is that leadership development is no longer "one size fits all." Although we do need to develop a leadership pipeline for our organization – one which pours in volunteers and spits out leaders – much of the training will need to be adjusted to the individual, and to the ever-changing culture. This is where the mentoring and coaching process will prove to be extremely valuable.

Those of us that have been around longer have learned how to play by the rules. We were taught that we had to pay if we wanted to play. Millennials, on the other hand, believe the rules are stupid and get in the way of progress. And in some instances they are right.

Never forget that they have a strong desire to make an impact. They just don't yet realize the price necessary to achieve this goal. Although it may be a frustrating process, God has called us to empower this generation. There is greatness in them and they are truly destined for great things. It is up to us to call it out of them, gently nurture their gifts and allow them to shine.

My experience is that Millennials greatly desire mentoring relationships with seasoned leaders. But in order for us to fill this position for them we will have to rely on God's wisdom and exhibit great patience. When it comes to developing Millennial leaders we have to realize that God has given us a plot of land with plenty of trees and a graphite mine. It is up to us to create pencils and paper.

Previous generations expected to start at the bottom and work their way up. They understood the need to *earn* the right to have a voice. But this "privileged" generation expects to have a voice as soon as they enter the doors. Their inexperience produces a lack of self-awareness. Many don't recognize either the range or the impact of their weaknesses. And most of them believe they innately know more than older generations.

Church leaders need to understand this chasm in expectations between the generations. If we want Millennials to step up to the plate, we need to be willing to give newcomers a voice sooner than we'd like. Complaining that they just don't get it doesn't help anyone. And demanding that they pay their dues will only cause them to go elsewhere.

We need to invite younger leaders – even unproven ones – to sit at the decision making table with us. We need to give them meaningful leadership roles, sometimes even before they're ready. And we have to allow them to fail. If we can teach them the value of failure – to learn from their mistakes – they will see that failure isn't fatal or futile. This is how they learn. And it's a much safer way to pay their dues than if they had to figure everything out alone.

Of course we need to be wise in how we do this. Young leaders need to learn that leadership empowerment is a process. It consists of delegation, inspection and debrief. We train them to lead and then give them the permission to do so. Along the way we check to make sure everything is flowing smoothly. If it's not, we have to fight the temptation to solve their problems for them. *They* need to figure it out *for themselves.* We, of course, can coach them by asking good questions. But they need to grow in their own problem-solving abilities.

123

Afterward we need to debrief them about their experience. Questions are powerful tools in the hands of a skilled mentor. But this needs to be done in the context of a relationship, not like a drill instructor. If we do it mechanically they will shut down. If we are wise we will learn from them too. We need to ask them questions such as:

- What went right?

- What went wrong?

- Was there anything you didn't see coming?

- What was different than your expectations?

- What was the hardest part of this experience?

- What did you learn?

- From what you learned, what is transferrable to other areas of leadership and ministry?

- What from this experience can you pass on to the people you will mentor?

These questions are invaluable as we coach young leaders. What I've learned is that our prepared question isn't always the most important one. It's often the follow-up question that brings insight and wisdom. In Jesus' mentoring process with His team it looked like this:

- "Who do people say I am?" *(Main question)*

- "But what about you? Who do you say that I am?"[95] *(Follow-up question)*

The Most Difficult Person To Lead

Of course we can never talk about leading others without discussing the importance of leading ourselves. It's been said over and over that the most difficult person to lead is yourself. This is absolutely true! We can't expect to attract disciplined people if we won't discipline ourselves. In order to lead others, especially other leaders, you have to grow your own leadership ability. You will never lead a stronger leader than yourself. They will grow frustrated and restless, and will either leave or cause trouble.

Pastor Scott Wilson writes:

> *A friend of mine created what he calls "The Negative One Differential Factor of Leadership" based on his observation that we are attracted to people who are farther along than we are in a given area. Because we are all continually growing, leaders don't attract and build people who rate higher than they do. So in terms of leadership, if I'm a seven on a scale of ten, I'll seek out someone who is an eight. And I'll be able to mentor someone who is a six or below.*[96]

If I want to attract a high-producing team of sevens or eights, I have to be a nine. Robin and I have noticed a number of pastors of large, growing churches that aren't great speakers. They do a good job, but we would normally expect pastors of large churches to be *exceptional* communicators. To our surprise, this isn't always the case. As we investigated what enabled them to grow such large churches, we kept coming to the same conclusion: they are great leaders.

Great leaders attract other great leaders to their team, which brings the potential for explosive growth. We have to be constantly growing in our leadership ability and passion. If not, we become what Dr. John Maxwell calls the "Leadership Lid" for our organization. No one in our organization will grow beyond us. If they do, as I said before, they will look elsewhere to find a stronger leader to serve.

So how do you grow your leadership ability? The first thing I would say is an old adage: Leaders are learners. No one grows automatically. It takes effort. You need to continually fill your mind and heart with material and relationships in the area you want to grow. This doesn't have to cost a fortune. There is a LOT of free material on the Internet, thanks to some very generous leaders. But I would also tell you that developing as a leader is so important that it is worth getting a part-time job just to pay for the materials.

You also need to invest in yourself by attending seminars and conferences. Dr. Gerald Brooks says there are intangible benefits to "being in the room" – in that learning atmosphere – which you won't get by just listening to the mp3s or watching the videos. It's important sometimes to be in the same room with great leaders.

I would encourage you to develop a relationship with a leader (or leaders) that is (are) on your level of leadership, one that is a little bit ahead you and one far ahead of you that are willing to invest in you. Each of these will be able to help you develop your leadership skills in different areas.

Any personal time you can spend with a great leader is well worth it. Make sure you don't waste their time. Come with a list of questions, the most important of which is: "What questions should I be asking you right now?" And for goodness sake, don't just talk... LISTEN! I remember a time when I was asked by a pastor to spend time with one of his leaders. As we were having dinner this guy dominated the conversation. He asked me a question and then proceeded to tell me the answer, or at least what he thought the answer should be. Because he so monopolized the conversation I never had the chance give him an answer. Don't be that guy!

Chapter 15
Vision Casting

Anyone that leads needs to be able to share the vision of what God has called the organization to become and to do. Pastor Andy Stanley calls this God's preferred future for your organization. Some are better at this than others. But every leader needs to be able to motivate his people in one way or another toward the sunset picture we discussed in Chapter 9.

Modeling The Vision

Pastor Chris Seay of Ecclesia Church in Houston, TX communicates by his attitude and actions that the homeless people his church reaches are no different than him, except that he happens to live in a house. He invites his church to truly do life together with the homeless in their community. Every Sunday after church many of their people, including the homeless, meet at a homeless shelter to eat together. They all take turns serving. He takes the lead in modeling the vision of his church.

Pastors need to lead their churches into what they want to see. A leader is, by definition, out in front. The leader needs to show his people what is important and what truly matters. He must help them avoid distractions that would pull them off course. He must continually bring people back to their God-given DNA. *(Please note that when I use the word "he" for pastor I mean it in a generic way to mean both men and women. I believe many people have greatly underestimated the role of women in our churches. But that is another book for another day!)*

Shane Duffey, the Creative Arts Pastor of Newspring Church in Anderson, SC said in a Perry Noble Leadership

Podcast, "The best way to train your leaders is to rub shoulders with them and think out loud." Isn't this what Jesus did? The Bible records Him doing life with twelve men, eleven of which would later go on to change the world by carrying out His mission to build the Church. Yes, there were others that followed, some quite closely. But these twelve – Peter, James and John in particular – went with Jesus everywhere.

Early on in my ministry career I learned that one of the best ways to invest in my leaders was to take them with me. Whether I went to the grocery, hardware or music store, as often as possible I took someone with me. This enabled me to learn their heart, and for them to catch mine. They began to understand what I saw, what I valued and how I thought. They began to sense what decisions I would make before I made them. And they caught my passion for our people.

Pastors are excellent at "faking it." Many are quite friendly on Sunday because it's their job, and it's expected of them. But then they are anti-social during the week, except when their job requires them to interact with their people. If we are called to pastor, Jesus expects us to shepherd our people.

I witnessed what this means while on a mission trip in the Romanian countryside. As I watched, a shepherd and his 50 or so sheep walked over the hill across from us. The shepherd would walk with his sheep to an open pasture. Every now and then he would speak to them in a comforting voice. Then after a while he moved on, all the while speaking to them. They stayed close to him, just as Jesus mentioned in John 15:1-5.

If we are called to be pastors, we must do life with our people. Shepherds smell like their sheep. We have to get to know them and allow them to get to know us. We need to share our lives with our people. Dr. John Maxwell says we need to "walk slowly through the crowd" just like Jesus did. He was willing to be interrupted because He truly valued people.[97]

I remember a time when the church where I worked experienced rapid growth. I had so many responsibilities I hadn't yet delegated that I was exhausted. I would run around before the church service practically ignoring the people – or worse, asking the obligatory, "How's it going?" but not really wanting an answer. God spoke to my heart very clearly one day. He instructed me to stop all the busy work and just BE with my people; to let whatever wasn't done stay undone. After all, the people are the reason we are there in the first place!

We are supposed to be the ones giving life, not ones living off of the energy/resources our people provide for us. Certainly we aren't so arrogant as to think that our Sunday sermons alone are good enough to meet our people's needs. We have to get close enough to our people to impart life to them. You can influence someone from a distance; but genuine life impact only happens up close.[98] True ministry impact is all about proximity.

It's too easy to hide behind our pulpits and wait for the people to come to us. But Jesus told us to GO (not wait). And Jesus said that we should go after the lost sheep.[99]

If we as pastors and leaders don't embrace and live out the vision, our people won't. We have to do exponentially more than we expect them to do.

Follow The Leader

If you're frustrated with your congregation, you need to look in the mirror. As Dr. John Maxwell often says, "We teach what we know, but we reproduce who we are."

Healthy pastors and leaders produce healthy churches. If pastors aren't growing spiritually, they won't grow their churches. None of the principles in this book will have much of an effect if the leadership of the church isn't healthy. Let me put it another way… unhealthy leaders create toxic churches.

Pastors, what are you personally doing to reinforce the culture you desire to see in your church? Are *you* growing spiritually? Are *you* having a daily devotional time? Are *you* really entering into worship on Sundays? Are *you* intentionally engaging with and inviting unchurched people to visit your church? Are *you* looking for opportunities to serve your neighbors? Are *you* involved in a small group?

Gone are the days of the untouchable pastors who swoop in on Sunday mornings just before the service begins and are escorted out the back before it ends. Jesus didn't have a Green Room (a private backstage room for the pastor and his entourage). Neither should we. Millennials are sick and tired of rock star pastors. They want the authentic, gritty, uncut version of us. That's where life connection really happens.

If Robin and I had not intentionally built relationships with the unchurched, our people wouldn't have either. They would not have brought their unchurched friends. Our church would not have attracted or connected with people that were far from God. And we would have failed in our primary mission. Connecting with people where they are is messy, inconvenient and complicated.[100] But that is absolutely where life change happens.

Had we not intentionally been generous and serving, our people would not have been either. Our church would not have gained the reputation as a church that served with no strings attached. And we would not have been given a wide open door to partner with a local grade school.

Had my family not been the first to arrive, the last to leave and the hardest working, our people would have simply done church as usual: only doing what is necessary, and even then, only when they were scheduled to serve. Instead, we created a culture of *ownership*: "This is MY church! I will do whatever necessary to make it work." There were quite a few Sundays that my family worked the hardest!

While in Europe, our family was able to go to Disneyland Paris. We loved it! The Disney culture is truly one of ownership. Disney is so focused on vision that it's *owned* by all 67,000 employees. Every one of them thinks like an owner and picks up trash. The value of keeping the park clean is so contagious, even guests will pick up trash if they see it lying around. That's a contagious strategy and value system.[101]

Staying true to the mission, vision and values is an uphill battle. You need to realize that everyone who comes to your church has an agenda.[102] Robin and I actually *prefer* to work with the unchurched. It's less difficult than working with churched people because they don't have any preconceived ideas of what a church is "supposed" to look like, sound like and act like. Actually, you just trade one set of problems for another because the unchurched still have their opinion of what your church should do for them when they come.

A pastor I've been coaching told me of a Facebook message he had read. The pastor of a church of 2,500 people surveyed his church members about what they liked and disliked. He also included the question, "What is the purpose of this church?" Over ¾ of the congregation answered something to the effect of, "To minister to me and my family." OUCH!!! Needless to say, this was disheartening, and it required a re-infusion of vision into the congregation. *The Gospel has never been about us!* It's about those that haven't even come through the church doors yet.

Keep Casting Vision

Pastor Andy Stanley of Northpoint Church in Alpharetta, GA gives us a clear and simple truth: "Vision leaks." We have to continually be filling our people with the vision. Dr. John Maxwell often says that a leader needs to recast the vision to his or her people every 21 days. If not, they will stray from what God has called their organization to be. We call this "mission drift."

We have to be creative in how we share the vision in order to keep it from growing stale. We need to continually saturate our people with our picture of the sunset. We must continue to tell real-life stories of people who are living out the vision, and those that have been impacted by it. As we do so we reveal what we consider worthy of celebration. It shows our people what a "win" looks like.

At Watermark the "face" of our Kids Church (and our outreach) was a young Muslim boy named Alex. He lived across the street from our church building. He came over to "help" us renovate the building for our opening service. He loved being a part of what was happening, and our team adopted him and his sister, Mimi, as honorary team members.

Our team members had name tags that we wore in the services. Alex and Mimi each got to wear one too.

Both of these kids gave their hearts to Jesus at our second service. They have only missed a handful of services since! They even dragged their mother and father with them to church as often as they could. We told and retold this ever-growing story about who Alex was before and after his encounter with Jesus. Because of stories like this our people understood exactly *why* we did what we did.

When we lived in Germany we would host a Superbowl party every year for our friends and neighbors. And every year I ended up having to explain the rules and strategies because most Germans understand soccer, not American Football. Every sport has rules to ensure everyone is playing the same game, and so that they do so safely and fairly. Can you imagine playing badminton with rugby rules? The paramedics on the sidelines would definitely earn their paychecks dealing with all the wounded!

Each sport also has short-term goals that help us determine whether or not we're making progress. In football it's the first down and the touchdown. In soccer it's scoring a goal. In baseball it's getting on base and scoring a run, or getting an opposing team's player out. In tennis it's the point, the game and the set. These help keep us on track and motivated as we advance toward our goal of winning.

Each sport also clearly defines what a win looks like. In golf it's having the lowest score. In football, soccer, baseball and basketball it's exactly the opposite. In auto racing it's crossing the finish line first. In swimming it's having the fastest time. In rugby it appears to be seeing how many of the other team's players you can send to the hospital.

Just as sporting events have goals and clearly defined wins, our churches must too. Our short- and long-term goals help us measure whether or not we're making progress. They keep us on track. And they show us when we're fulfilling the mission of the game – when we're winning.

We have to define the win for our leadership teams. If we don't clearly define the win we can't complain about the results. What is recognized and rewarded gets repeated, so we need to make sure everyone knows what is important.

So what does a win look like in your context? Is it having a large weekend crowd? Is it the number of small groups, or the percentage of your people involved in them? Is it the number of baptisms? Or is it the number of 2nd, 3rd or 4th time visitors?

Whatever your goals, you need a way to track forward progress. You need to know the total attendance for each service, and the ratio of adults to kids. You should know how many visitors attended, and how many returned. How many visitors are you moving into your membership or spiritual formation pathways? How many of your members are actively serving (volunteering) in the church? In the community? How many of the people that got through your membership pathway move into serving positions? How soon? And, of course, you need to track income and expenses.

As we define our wins and goals we also need to show our people how these goals relate to our vision and values. Pastor Andy Stanley communicates very clearly to his leaders the goal for any weekend service: Getting people to come back the following weekend. *Why* is this so important? He says they aren't able to disciple a person that isn't engaged in their church.

One more important thing to remember about vision: it chooses our people for us. Dr. Gerald Brooks says your vision and values are like a magnet. They will attract some people and repel others. He was once asked how he had grown his church to 4,000 people. He responded that you have to be willing to run off 12,000 people. You have to know what you're called to do and who you're called to reach. Never let anything distract you from those two things.

We won't reach everyone. We're not called to do it and certainly not equipped for it. But if we'll focus on those we *are* called to reach, people from other walks and stages of life will come be a part of our churches as well.

Quality Control

So what did a win look like for Watermark? Below is a *partial* list. I'm including these so you'll see how this works in the real world in real time. I have also included some questions for each point that we used for quality control. We couldn't leave something as important as a *win* up to chance.

Our wins:

- Our core values are so embodied by our Team and our church members that they are evident to visitors. *If I ask a visitor to tell me what we value based on their observations, are they able to come up with at least two or three of our core values?* By the way, this is one of the reasons why Jesus came – to be an incarnational example of God's value system.

- We attract new visitors (especially unchurched visitors) – This helps us gauge how effective our marketing & personal invitations are. *Are visitors coming on a regular basis? How did they hear about us? How many visitors did our team identify? How many of them actually went to Info Booth? Were they engaged in conversation and asked to give us their contact information? Were they given information on our small groups? Which of our team members connected with them? Who will do follow-up, and when?* All of our visitors were contacted within 24 hours. If an unchurched visitor truly feels *welcomed*, he or she will be more willing to hang around afterward. Some US churches use the term "guest" in place of "visitor" because they feel it is more inviting. To a German the term "visitor" wasn't offensive or problematic so we used it.

- Relational connection (to God and to others) happens – This adds value to the visitor's life. *Are people warmly welcomed, offered a cup of coffee and invited into a conversation? Do they hang out after the service and engage in conversation with others?* We didn't get upset if they didn't give us their contact info. In a Post-Christian setting people don't trust churches. We still gave them a gift for visiting.

o Another way we measured this was by determining how many people answered the invitation to either commit or recommit their life to Christ at the end of our service. If we didn't see regular numbers of people making commitments to Christ we knew were mainly attracting believers – often from other churches – and that we needed to change something.

- Visitors come back – We can't disciple people that don't attend. If they return it tells us that we did something right the last time they visited, and that they sensed a value in what we offered them. And if they brought a friend back with them we know we had a BIG WIN! *Who came back this week? Did they bring anyone with them? Which of our team members connected with them? Did they say why they returned? Was their last visit the first time they ever attended a church? Have they connected with any of our small groups?*

  o As I mentioned before, Andy Stanley's main goal in a weekend service is to get people to come back. Permanent life change rarely happens through a one-time event!

- Our staff and team take ownership and initiative… our people lead! – We focused on equipping and empowering our team members and volunteers to lead and serve. During our pre-service team meeting we gave them permission to come up with creative solutions to any problems or questions they would face that day. We had drilled the vision and values into them and this was their chance to flesh it out. *Who took initiative this week? Did someone do something to "own" the vision? Did any of the staff express their appreciation? How can we celebrate this as a team?* We always sent some sort of message thanking our people when they displayed ownership and initiative.

  o A quick note: Be careful how you show your appreciation. We don't want our people to feel that they are doing something for *us*. We want them to feel the joy of being a part of a team of people working toward a common goal. We thanked our people for jumping in and taking on the vision as their own.

- Things are done with excellence – We defined this as doing the best we can with what we have. It is not the same as perfection. We need to assume that there is always a better, faster, cheaper and more efficient way to do things. We may not have discovered it yet, but it's there. And when someone finds a creative way to make things better we need to celebrate. *Who embodied the spirit of excellence this week? Did our staff say something to them yet? How can we celebrate this as a team?*

  o Questions we can ask our staff and team to encourage this mindset: *How can we do _____ better, faster, cheaper or more efficiently and effectively? Are we inviting our creative, out-of-the-box problem-solvers to help us find solutions? Has anyone asked other churches how they are solving this problem, or what they are doing to improve this area?*

I asked one pastor how he did quality control on their "visitor experience". He answered, "People vote with their feet and their wallets. As long as we have both of those we know the vision is working."

That's not good enough for me. It leaves too much up to chance. By the time it shows up in feet and wallets we will have lost some momentum. I need to have quantitative and qualitative feedback if I'm going to navigate my church toward God's vision for us. I have to be able to measure if we're doing a good job of attracting and welcoming people that are far from God or are spiritually disconnected.

I even asked a few of the unchurched people I met in Freiburg if they would visit our church and give me honest feedback afterward over lunch – my treat. This gave me a chance to invite an unchurched person to our church, to invest in a relationship with them and to get some quality control feedback at the same time. I always asked pastors and leaders of other churches that visited our services what they could tell about our core values based upon what they had observed.

We have to assume that when a person visits our church it may be their "last chance":

- "I'm going to give God one last chance to speak to me."

- "I'm only going to church with my mom because she keeps bugging me, but after this, I'm done."

- "I'm at the end of my rope. God, if you're there, this is your last chance to speak to me."

- "God, if you don't speak to us today we're going to the divorce lawyer tomorrow."

We only have one chance to make a good first impression, and to help people experience God's love and grace. We need to use it wisely! As Pastor Andy Stanley says, "I can't make people fall in love with Jesus, but I can arrange some dates."

Chapter 16
Developing Your Leadership Team

Anything that God calls you to do will be beyond your abilities. God-sized dreams are always bigger than one person's abilities. You will never be able to accomplish them by yourself. If you want to build anything significant – if you want to leave a true legacy – you're going to *have* to empower others. This is especially true when it comes to building a church.

Choosing Your Key Leaders

Of course when you start a church you welcome "whosoever will" to help you. You need people of all skill levels. But eventually you should work toward finding those that are able to empower others. As your leaders develop you need to search out those that can lead other leaders. This isn't playing favorites. It's positioning our people for maximum Kingdom impact.

Never underestimate the power of a personal invitation. People that would be great leaders for your church will often already be leading in a civic or business capacity. Ask these leaders to get more involved and to leverage their gifts to build God's Kingdom. High capacity leaders don't respond to cattle calls; they respond to a tap on the shoulder and a personal invitation.

Casey Graham says churches fail in this area because they are simply looking for people to fill in an organizational chart. Most churches are only looking for warm bodies. They ask people to serve with their *backs* and not their *heads*. High capacity leaders in your church (remember: these are often business owners and leaders) are looking for a problem to solve not a hole to fill.[103]

When we started meeting with our Launch Team we began to look for those that had the ability to lead others. In the context of working to get the building ready for our first service, we observed how people reacted in the team dynamic. We were, of course, thankful for *all* the amazing people God brought to our Team. But we kept hearing John Maxwell's mantra in our ears: "Everything rises and falls on leadership." If our church was going to explode out of the starting blocks, it would be because of a great group of leaders. Robin and I simply weren't capable of doing everything.

We began to train everyone on our Launch Team to lead, but we invested in some more than others. Leaders are like the cream in raw milk… they rise to the top. And that is exactly what happened. One of the things we noticed was that many of our Launch Team members were untrained leaders with lots of raw talent. They had a true pioneering spirit, which is why they were drawn to the opportunity of starting something new. We realized it was our God-given responsibility to bring out the best in them and allow them to use their gifts and passion for Kingdom purposes.

Leading leaders isn't easy. I've heard it likened to herding cats. But if you'll train, empower and release your people to lead, you'll see a HUGE payoff!

I first learned about the Parieto Principle from John Maxwell. In the early 20th century, Vilfredo Parieto, an Italian economist, came up with a mathematical formula to explain the disparity of wealth that he observed and measured in his country. His 80/20 principle actually applies to most areas in life. It's actually quite simple: The top 20% of your _____ (people, financial investments, time, efforts) will produce 80% of the results of your organization. In choosing leaders we don't look for *results* as much as we do the leadership initiative and ability, which will *produce* the results. We sought out the top 20% of our people (as far as leadership capacity and potential) and invested heavily in them.

In churches, pastors often try to make everything fair. But the Pareto Principle teaches us how to get the greatest return on our investment. Time and energy are a commodity that pastors and church planters often find in short supply. Understanding this, it is best to invest the lion's share of your time in your top producers.

Choosing one person over another or investing in one more than another doesn't sound fair to us, especially in church circles. But if we'll go back to Jesus' model of leadership development we'll see plainly that He made no apologies for spending more time with certain people than with others. He didn't seem to care about what was fair. He was more interested in fulfilling His mission.

- All four of Jesus' biographers – we know them as the Gospel writers Matthew, Mark, Luke and John – reveal that Jesus chose twelve men and appointed them to be apostles (the Greek word for apostle means "sent ones"). Their mission was "to be with Him, that He might send them out."[104]

- Though huge crowds followed Him, He only chose 70 men to send out on mission.[105]

- Even among the disciples Jesus had an inner circle of three – Peter, James and John. He took these three everywhere.[106]

- And out of the three, John obviously thought he was Jesus' favorite. He referred to himself as "the disciple Jesus loved" six times in his own Gospel account.

With this in mind, we knew we should invest heavily in some key people. But even among those that had great leadership potential we looked for a few crucial attributes in those we chose as our main leaders:

- Positive attitude – Do they see possibilities or just problems? Do their words give life, or do they just complain? *Without a positive attitude the other qualities don't matter much. If they don't have the right attitude, their influence will drain the team. I would rather have someone with a good attitude than the most talented leader in the world.*

- Influence – Do others follow them?

- Initiative – Do they need to be told what to do?

- Dependable – Do they follow through on assignments and commitments?

- Integrity – Are they honest and reliable?

- Affinity – Do they "gel" with us and with the others in our leadership development circle?

- Energy – Do they have the necessary energy to give life to those around them?

- Secure – Are they comfortable in their own skin? Are they self-aware of both strengths and weaknesses? *Insecure leaders are dangerous! If they can't let people around them shine, the organization will never grow beyond them. It will never become what God intended it to be.*

- Courage – Are they afraid of confrontation? *Confrontation is an unpleasant necessity in leadership. On the other hand, if a person enjoys confrontation too much they might misuse their influence and abuse people.*

- Hard working – Do they pitch in and help or do they just like telling others what to do?

- Team player – Do they play well with others? *We don't have time to deal with all the drama that a "diva" (a "prima donna" who acts overly entitled) brings, no matter how talented they are. I ignored some warning signs with one diva and it ended up costing us needless stress and influence with other leaders on the team.*

- Time – Do they have enough free time for us to be able to train them?

Let me add that you will make mistakes in this area. We certainly did. And the process will be messy. Developing people always is. Think about the different stages of *your* spiritual, emotional, social and physical development. It probably wasn't all nice and neat. Even though Jesus invested three years of His life in His twelve disciples, one of them didn't make it to the end. Those that did were often fighting among themselves over who was the most important – even as they walked down the road with Jesus!

You can easily find a more on this topic in some of the exceptional leadership materials found in the Appendix at the end of this book. We've listed some leadership resources that have been invaluable to us as we've worked through the leadership development process. There are many others that we have gleaned from, but these are the ones that have made the greatest impact in our lives.

Situational Leadership

It seems our entire civilization is built upon the concept of positional leadership. With a recognized position or title comes power and authority. If a person in a position of authority says it can't be done, then people assume it can't be done. This is certainly the case in Germany. But if you're going to build anything of value you have to be willing to buck this system from time to time.

In Germany we heard the phrase, "It can't be done" regurgitated on an almost daily basis. We were often told "no" by those in authority, and by those that didn't want to rock the boat or invest the effort into doing something new. We learned to ask if the thing was truly *impossible* or if it just hadn't been done before. Then we asked the person to help us think through ways around the roadblock. Sometimes we asked if the person with whom we were speaking even had the authority to tell us "yes." If not, we asked to speak with someone who did.

Situational leadership is all about seeing a problem and taking the initiative to solve it. Most people in our world are followers. They would love to do something of consequence, something that has lasting value. But they don't know how. Or they are too afraid to try it themselves. Situational leaders realize that someone has to go first.

One afternoon Jesus told His followers to take their boat and go over to the other side of the Sea of Galilee. They obeyed and set out. As they were out in the middle of the lake, a violent storm set in. As they were fighting the wind and the waves Jesus came to them walking on the water. Actually, He was about to walk past their boat when Peter yelled out, "Master, if it's really you, call me to come to you on the water."

Jesus said, "Come on." Then Peter did something absolutely crazy. He got out of the boat and walked toward Jesus on the water.

Maybe you know the rest of the story... Peter did well at first, but he started looking around at the wind and the waves and began to freak out. It says he began to sink. I'm not sure which one I find more amazing, that Peter actually walked on the water or that he *began* to sink. In all my time on this planet I've never seen anyone begin to sink.

Anyway, Jesus grabbed Peter's hand *before* he went under the water and walked him back to the boat. He challenged Peter for his lack of faith.[107]

When most Christians talk about this story they point out how Peter failed, and how important it is to focus on Jesus in the midst of distractions. But I see another principle at play here. Peter wasn't alone in that boat. There were eleven other disciples with him. *But he was the only one that got out of the boat!* And because he took a risk, he was the only person, besides Jesus, who knows what it's like to walk on water! Situational leaders are willing to get out of the boat, even if they have to do so alone. This is the type of person we sought out to help us lead – and who we trained our key leaders to look for in the second and third generation of leaders.

Training Your Team

The goal of training your team isn't to *reproduce* yourself, as many have said. This implies that you will create a bunch of "Mini-Me's" (as Austin Powers named his protégé). We are called to *replace* ourselves. Rather than creating carbon copies of ourselves, God expects us to help our leaders discover *their* gifts and *their* own style of leadership. Once they have a handle on that, we need to encourage them to use their unique gifts and passion to lead others and solve problems.

I've already outlined how we injected *our* DNA into our Launch Team. But there were some other ways we intentionally invested in our people, especially our key leaders:

We formed a group of four of our strongest leaders and started teaching them leadership principles weekly. We met every Thursday for about 90 minutes at a coffee shop downtown. Especially right before we launched it seemed as if we didn't have time for this, but we knew this was the most important investment we would make in our church. All four went on to become staff members. We required each of them to select and invest in other leaders as well.

We shared our connections/access. We exposed our key leaders to other great leaders and to leadership materials that impacted us. We created opportunities for them to attend church planting roundtables, Bible school classes and local pastoral alliance meetings. They also came with us to minister to a woman that had just lost everything in a fire, to meet with church members who needed a listening ear and to have lunch with community influencers. We purchased books and materials for them that would inspire them and help them develop their passion and skills.

We asked about their personal lives. It was important to us to not just know them organizationally, but personally. They needed to know that we cared for them as people, and not just for what they could add to our team. We began our staff meetings with everyone quickly sharing about their week and any prayer requests they had. It may seem a bit "touchy-feely" – especially to bottom-line people – but it proved quite effective for us.

We fed them and paid for countless cups of coffee. This simple act of generosity speaks volumes. Your people need to see you being generous with your time and your resources. Some pastors believe they don't have the money for this. But if you had to pay volunteers for all the work they do, how much would *that* cost you? Paying for snacks or meals is a cheap way to thank your volunteers for all the effort they give. If you don't have enough money to be generous you probably need to do some more fundraising.

We paid them with vision. I talk a lot about our team and staff, but it's important to note that no one at our church was paid. We were all volunteers. It may be harder to run a church with all volunteers, but we have to make sure that there is payment of some kind. We pay our volunteers with vision. Everyone – especially a Millennial – wants to feel that their efforts matter, that they are a part of something significant. When we fill them with vision and celebrate successes that part of their God-given need for significance is satisfied.

We focused our team training on situational leadership. The German system is permission based. So I told them in every pre-service meeting that I trusted them to make on-the-spot decisions (without having to get permission) based on the vision and values of the church. The German system is "no" based. The easy answer is always, "No, we can't do that." But we trained our people to look for ways to say 'yes' – to make things happen. Just because it hadn't been done before didn't necessarily make it wrong. And we celebrated when someone took initiative and ownership.

We shared our expectation that everyone was to "take someone along with him or her." We piggybacked off the German job training apprenticeship system. We expected anyone serving – whether in Kids Church, serving coffee or greeting – to find someone else to do it with them. One of our mantras was, "No one serves alone." The apprentice then shadowed the person serving until they were comfortable with the task, at which point the person serving stepped into the shadowing role. Eventually the former apprentice found their own apprentice and the process repeated itself. This proved to be quite effective.

In the German system, people work toward gaining a leadership position. Once you "arrive" you don't let go of your position for any reason. We had to counter this with a LOT of teaching and modeling. We explained that leaders who are able to raise up others to take over their job are leaders that *we can't afford to lose*. In other words, *if you replace yourself you're irreplaceable to us!*

One of the main questions we kept asking was, "Who are you empowering?" And along with it was, "Are you actively scouting/recruiting new talent?" We had to continually reinforce this so they didn't lose the vision of developing others. We explained that this was a part of the discipleship process.

People will visit your church to see if it offers them something. Of course we want to retain every visitor God sends us. If we are successful and they start coming back, it's important to try to discover their gifts/passion in order to find a place for them to use their gifts to serve. Their passion may not actually fit within your vision/values. That's not a problem. Just help them find another organization that will take advantage of their gifts. After all, it's not about growing your church, but about growing God's Kingdom. If you are open-handed (not jealous/controlling) with your people, they will notice and be remarkably loyal to you.

We had pre-service meetings with the entire Launch Team. These were 15 - 20 minutes long, concluding 30 minutes before people started arriving. Our meetings consisted of three things:

- A quick rundown of who/what was happening that Sunday.

- A short leadership or vision thought relating to one of the four core values.

- Prayer for the service, our visitors, our altar calls and our volunteers.

We gave them real opportunities. We provided speaking opportunities to our staff. We had them speak in pre-service meetings, team meetings and in the services. We eased them into it. We taught them how to prepare a message, had them preach their message to the rest of the staff (before doing so publicly) and then offered feedback. We started them out emceeing the service, and then had them do the announcements and offering. Once they were ready we had them teach a message in the service. The most important part of this process was the debrief afterwards.

We asked questions. If you study the leadership style of Jesus, you'll notice that His main form of leadership training was to ask questions. This happened during His teaching and in debriefing sessions. We live in a world where those in authority give answers. But Jesus asked questions. Why? Asking gets people to think. Never underestimate the power of good questions.

My main goal is not to get my people thinking like I do, but instead to get them to process information and situations with our mission, vision and values in mind. I don't want my leaders, especially my key leaders, acting like employees. Employees simply do what they're told. Managers go further – they begin to think like I think. But I don't want them to stop at this level either. I want them taking ownership. This will only happen if I teach them to see what I see and then process what they see through the filter of our mission, vision and values. And then I need to empower them to make decisions based on their conclusions... not just thinking, "What would Jon do?" They need to be empowered to do it *their* way, as long as it fits within our mission, vision, values and strategy.

If you want your people to start thinking like owners instead of employees, you need to invite their input. Placing value upon their observations, opinions and suggestions shows that you respect their *hearts and minds*, not just what they can *do*. Even if you don't act on their suggestions, people need to feel heard. As I said before, we can't afford to value people's backs, but not their brains.

On the other hand, the German culture places a high value on consensus. Everyone expects to have a say in every matter affecting the church. They not only expect to have a say; they expect that everyone's vote counts equally. While there are some benefits to building consensus (checks and balances), you need to understand that consensus is a dream-killer! Pastor Carey Nieuwhof says the quickest way to kill momentum is to give everyone a vote.[108]

I believe a pastor should have a council of people within his church that he can consult on matters of importance. He should also have a group of overseers that hold him accountable for his actions. If he is smart he will rely on both when it comes to major decisions. But he needs to have the right to make the final decision. *(Again, I mean both men and women when I refer to pastoring.)*

Let me give you a final thought about training your team. I realize this is a well-used leadership mantra, but it's still true: **You need to inspect what you expect**. Why? If people know they will be held accountable for something they are more likely to put extra effort into it. It is human nature that what is recognized and rewarded gets repeated.

The Importance of Written Job Descriptions

If we had to do it all over again we would probably bring written job descriptions into our leadership structure sooner. One of our mantras in the early days of our church was "everyone does everything."

Because of the school calendar most of our Launch Team didn't get involved until 6 - 8 weeks before we started. During this time we were also attempting to turn an old dirty warehouse into a church building, and do so on a shoestring budget. This means our team had to do all the work ourselves. We knew we could either focus our energy on being highly organized or on developing strong relational bonds. Of course we chose the latter. As we worked on the building and grounds together the relationships grew. One of the comments we often received from visitors was, "You all *really do* enjoy each other and what you're doing, don't you?" We had succeeded in making our church a fun place to serve.

We did select people to serve as area leaders (kids, translation, coffee, sound, hospitality, etc.) but we rotated the rest of the team in other areas. One exception was in Kids Church where we did a lot of training and focused on getting a fixed rotation of good teachers. In every other area of the church (except the music team) we rotated our team members into the different serving positions in order to see where people's passion and skills intersected.

After we started plugging people into the area where they would be serving we helped them form teams. And we asked the area leaders and teams to create their own job descriptions. This worked, but it was a bit like brushing a cat the wrong way. Trying to add structure to a free flowing, make-it-up-as-we-go organization felt a bit stifling.

Why are job descriptions so important? They enable us to share clear expectations with those we lead. Because we have it in writing we are able to do this in a way that is non-threatening. We are simply letting our team know what is expected of them and setting appropriate boundaries.

If they fail to meet the agreed-upon expectations it gives us a legitimate way to bring confrontation or correction, if necessary. We can bring them back to the job description and show them how they didn't meet the necessary expectations. And we can do so in a respectful, relational way because we had *earned* the relationship first. And when they do meet expectations we can affirm the work they are doing much better than just, "Good job, dude."

We need to remember the goal of confrontation: the restoration of relationship. When one team member fails to accomplish a necessary task, the entire team suffers. This creates stress and strain on working and interpersonal relationships. Confrontation, when done correctly, allows us to restore these relationships to more than just a functional level. Lack of confrontation breeds distrust among team members.

There is a big difference between a job description and a policy. It's always easier to create policy than to deal with a person directly.[109] Policies are simply rules. They enable us to set clear-cut boundaries, but they don't encourage relationship, ownership or thought. Rules simply require obedience. They don't necessitate us "getting our hands dirty" by dealing with uncomfortable conversations.

Job descriptions, however, deal with our expectations for our people. They establish boundaries, and enable us to evaluate a person's performance against a set of clear expectations. They should also encourage initiative. They should empower people to do more than just cross one more thing off of their to-do list.

Policy says, "Answer the phone *like this*: 'Thank you for calling Watermark Church. My name is _____. How may I help you?'"

A job description goes more like this: "We expect our volunteers to handle all of our customers respectfully, to have a positive, can-do attitude and a pleasant demeanor." This encourages our people to be creative in their implementation of the expectation.

Sometimes it is necessary to create policy – especially in the case of a recurring problem. Repetitive problems reveal a lack of clear communication on our part. But creating policy should be the exception, not the rule

Chapter 17
Finding Your Elisha

Before moving back to the USA our family was able to do one final European road trip. We took the ferry from Calais, France to Dover, England and spent the night there. The next day we toured the Dover Castle. It was awesome! On the walls of the castle church we saw some Crusader graffiti scrawled into the church wall. These men wanted to leave some sort of mark on the world before heading out into battle.

It got me thinking about our mortality. We are not guaranteed our next breath. No one really knows what lies ahead. Before we depart we want to leave some sort of legacy that will live on after we're gone. We only have a few short years in which to impact our world, hopefully for the better.

Some men build grandiose monuments to show how important and impressive they are (were). Others scrawl graffiti over those monuments, as a small way of leaving something behind. This graffiti "shortcut" leaves people more disgusted than impressed. In our digital world graffiti looks more like online criticism in blog posts and articles. It has always been easier to deface what someone else has done than to build something that matters.

Men and women of honor build something significant. Small minded men and women seek to tear it down. But great men and women realize that the way to leave behind a true legacy is to invest your life into serving others and empowering them to succeed.

Succession Planning

Unfortunately the clock is counting down for all of us. We will all eventually leave this world. What will happen to the churches and ministries we've built after we're gone? We should continually be thinking of who will carry on our mission. Any good leader always does!

We have to be constantly mindful of what we can do to develop and prepare the next generation of spiritual leaders. If we don't prepare them the Church will suffer. If you were to hand your church over to the young leaders you have right now, how do you think they would handle it? Would they be prepared or would they struggle?

Everything we build will eventually end up in someone else's hands. If we prepare the next generation of leaders to step in our legacy will continue, and what we've built will hopefully grow. If not, it will crumble. In the Old Testament history books we see this pattern play out time and again.

Dr. Gerald Brooks says that the shelf life of a church is 20 years. After 20 years the leadership, vision and direction of a church has usually become so inward focused that it fails to make any real impact on its community or its people. It has simply become a religious organization. The only way to change this is to become intentional about empowering the next generation of leaders and then to hand them the reigns.

Elijah's story makes for an interesting read. God gave him a mission: to call the nation of Israel back from its apostasy. King Ahab and Queen Jezebel had led Israel into worshipping Baal and Ashtoreth (the gods of Israel's neighbors), even to the point of sacrificing their children in the fire. Now, more than ever, Israel needed a true leader – a man of God – to step in!

You can read the story in 1 Kings 17 - 18. God supernaturally used Elijah to dramatically call the nation back to Him. But in 1 Kings 19 we find Elijah running for his life. Queen Jezebel put a price on his head so he went into hiding. When God appeared to him he complained that he was the only God-loyal person left. He whined and asked God to kill him.

To the reader this sounds incredibly dramatic and almost comical. But haven't we all felt like this? God calls us to something amazing. We put our heart and soul into building something (a church, perhaps), but no one else really gets it. It seems that we are the only ones that truly eat, sleep, breathe and bleed the vision. We end up feeling all alone.

It doesn't have to be like this. God calls us to *share* the ministry. He wants us to train the next generation of leaders – not just to help us, but to actually take the reins and lead our churches into the future. Let's see what He said to Elijah in response to his whining.

> *The Lord said to him, "Go back the way you came, and go to the Desert of Damascus. When you get there, anoint Hazael king over Aram. Also, anoint Jehu son of Nimshi king over Israel, and anoint Elisha son of Shaphat from Abel Meholah to succeed you as prophet. Jehu will put to death any who escape the sword of Hazael, and Elisha will put to death any who escape the sword of Jehu. Yet I reserve seven thousand in Israel—all whose knees have not bowed down to Baal and whose mouths have not kissed him."*

> *1 Kings 19:15-18*

God tells Elijah to delegate parts of the mission to others, and then to train Elisha as his successor. Then God tells him to quit whining. In essence He says, "You're not the only one. Get up and get going!" Been there; done that!

God's call on Elijah's life was so big it took three other men to complete it. And God had specifically called Elisha to succeed him. Elisha was to finish what God had started through Elijah's ministry. Who is called to succeed you?

Why We Don't Raise Up Leaders

Not all leaders train the next generation to step into their shoes. It's not a given. Even leaders of large organizations fail at this. There are a myriad of reasons. Let's look at a few.

The most common reason is that we let fear or selfishness keep us from raising up people to replace us. This is simply insecurity on our part. We feel that if we train someone else, they will take our job and we'll become redundant, or worse: obsolete. Many of us are so tied to our position that it becomes our identity. And if we were to lose our position we'd forfeit our identity, which is our security.

Or we don't trust that someone else can lead as well or with the same amount of passion that we have. After all, it's *our* blood sweat and tears that have brought the organization this far. Why should we hand it off to someone else that will just screw it up?

How small-minded this reasoning is! We need to remember that God has given us leadership abilities in order to invest in others. God gives us increase in finances, connections, abilities, etc. so that we can have a positive impact on the world around us.[110]

Some leaders have been burned by those they've trained. They invested their time, heart and wisdom into someone, but the person ended up serving in another area or leaving altogether. This leaves a leader feeling betrayed, or that they've just wasted their time. Because of this many leaders just shut down. We have to become more Kingdom-minded than this!

Make no mistake; it will happen. You will invest in someone that ends up going to another church or ministry. It's frustrating and sometimes it's downright painful. But there will be other times when someone comes to us that has already been trained, that someone else has invested their time, heart and wisdom into. In order to have trained leaders come alongside me to help, I first need to invest in other leaders, regardless of whether they stay or go. Paul told the Galatian church that if they wanted to reap a harvest they first had to plant some crops.[111]

Sometimes leaders don't want to invest the time and energy necessary to produce leaders. Leadership development is extremely energy- and time-intensive. It's messy and emotionally exhausting. It is one of the hardest things you'll ever do. But the payoff is huge!

I am so thankful for the many leaders that invested in me along the way, even when it seemed as if nothing was penetrating my thick skull! They made an impact in my life. And I am a part of their legacy, even if they don't know it.

The Price You'll Pay

If you, as the pastor, can't seem to adjust to the culture of your local community you probably need to bring some fresh blood into the leadership of your church. Allow the younger generation to take the reins. If you allow them to lead they will surprise you. IT WILL BE SCARY! They think differently, but that's a good thing. As long as they have your DNA in them – not just memorized, but flowing through their soul – they can breathe new life into a declining or plateaued church. Besides, this is the only way young leaders will gain the experience necessary to produce at a high level.

You will probably lose members that have grown comfortable with your leadership and the status quo. But as we've already said, you grow a church by choosing whom you're willing to lose. If you want to reach those that are outside your church's walls, you'll have to be willing to lose those that have grown comfortable and complacent.

Why do people leave? Most of the time it's because they don't like change. As your church grows it changes. People will always view your church according to the size and feel that it was when they first came.[112] A church of 50 people offers more access to the pastor and leaders than a church of 250, and WAY more access than a church of 2500. A smaller church offers a family atmosphere that larger churches have a hard time replicating.

Let's be honest... watching people you love and pray for leave your church is scary, especially if they leave as a group! Any good pastor will have relationships and a history with his people. Bringing in new leadership risks having people that have persevered with you through the different stages and struggles of your church walk away. This means losing people that trust and believe in you. And possibly the scariest of all, losing people means losing their financial support.

The Payoff

But as I said, the payoff is well worth it. You'll be preparing the next generation of spiritual leaders. You'll be doing exactly what Jesus commanded all believers (especially spiritual leaders) to do: make disciples.

As I said before, anything God has called you to do is much bigger than you. It *will* require others to complete it. The Bible is full of examples: Moses & Joshua, David & Solomon, Elijah & Elisha, Jesus and His disciples, Paul & Timothy. Leadership is a long-distance relay, not a sprint. You will need to hand off the baton or your mission will go unfulfilled.

I love what the Apostle Paul said of King David, "He did God's will during his lifetime. Then he died and was buried beside his ancestors."[113] This is *my* dream! I want to fully complete the work God has called me to do before my time here is finished. And then I want to hand the baton to someone that will go farther than I ever could have, that will take the mandate God has given me to the next level.

This is exactly what David did for his son, Solomon. He taught him commonsense wisdom and a reverence for God.[114] He set Solomon up financially, organizationally and with strategic alliances and treaties. He gathered the resources and left detailed instructions for the construction of the Temple. And before David died, he publicly handed off the leadership of the nation of Israel to Solomon.

At Watermark we began recruiting and developing leaders even before we launched our church because we felt God wanted us to be a church-planting church. We knew this would require a LOT of good leaders. Empowering leaders paid off richly when our family needed to go back to the USA for eight months. This furlough happened as our church began its third year. The leaders we trained to pastor our future church plants stepped in to lead in our absence.

Get Into Position

So Christ himself gave the apostles, the prophets, the evangelists, the pastors and teachers, to equip his people for works of service, so that the body of Christ may be built up until we all reach unity in the faith and in the knowledge of the Son of God and become mature, attaining to the whole measure of the fullness of Christ.

Ephesians 4:11-13

Our responsibility as pastors is to train the people God sends us to do the "works of service." But because we fail to train our people, we end up doing everything ourselves. If you do everything yourself you are *robbing* your people of the God-given privilege and excitement of using their gifts. Your people are gifts that God has given you. And just like the natural gifts He has invested in you, He expects you to develop them and get them into the game.

Because of our natural gifting and experience there were many things Robin and I could probably have done better than the people on our team. But we chose instead to train and empower our people. We released them to use their creativity and passion to build God's Kingdom, both inside our church and in other areas. And they surprised us with their creativity, passion and ability to get things done. It was awesome!

Jim Collins suggests that one major key to becoming a great organization is getting the wrong people off of the bus, and getting the right people on the bus and into the right seats.[115]

Dr. Dean Radtke of the Ministry Leadership Institute likens a pastor to an orchestra conductor. In his analogy, the conductor's job is to make sure everyone performs in sync with each other. Those on the far left of the orchestra can't hear or see what's going on over on the far right side, so they have to watch the conductor in order to play in step with everyone else. She is the one up front and all eyes are on her.

But what if she notices that the tuba player keeps missing a note. Picture the scene… she leaves the stage and runs over to sit beside the tuba player. While the song continues to be played, the conductor takes the tuba from him and shows him how to do it correctly.

But wait!!! She also hears a trumpeter hold out a note too long. She rushes over to take the trumpet away from her, saying, "Let me show you how it's done," as she plays for the next few minutes.

And then she realizes the triangle player just missed a "ding." She drops the trumpet and hurries over to the triangle player. After chewing him out for missing a note, she proceeds to play the triangle for the next few minutes.

As she rushes from instrument to instrument the entire orchestra is getting more and more out of sync with each other. Why? Because the conductor is out of position! Her job is to remain up front. Yes, she needs to train the orchestra, but not *during* the performance. If she doesn't do *her job*, the entire orchestra suffers.

In the same way, a pastor or ministry area leader needs to be coordinating the volunteers as *they* do the work. *They* are the ones actually serving. *They* are the ones that are actually ministering to the people. And *they* should be the ones getting the credit. A great leader takes the blame for the team's mistakes and gives them the credit for successes.

Chapter 18
Everything Counts

Every leader has been tempted to measure his or her worth by a number, whether it's the number of members, visitors, small groups, dollars in the offering or kids in Kids Church. But we can never afford to allow numbers to determine our value. We matter because God calls us His own. And what we do for Him is simply a response to His generosity to us and to the call He has placed on our lives.

Having said that, numbers *are* important. They allow us to gauge what is happening in our churches. And they allow us to effectively plan for the future.

Numbers Matter

"Every number has a name. Every name has a story. Every story matters deeply to God."

Perry Noble

Anyone who has even given a perfunctory reading of the Book of Acts has probably noticed how often the number of people that were added to the Church was recorded. It occurs several times. Luke, the writer of the Book of Acts, felt it was important to chronicle the growth of the church. Let's look at it:

- Acts 1:15 - …<u>a group numbering about a hundred and twenty</u>.

- Acts 2:41 - and <u>about three thousand were added to their number</u> that day.

- Acts 2:47 - And the Lord <u>added to their number daily</u> those who were being saved.

- Acts 4:4 - But <u>many</u> who heard the message believed; so <u>the number of men who believed grew to about five thousand.</u>

- Acts 5:14 - Nevertheless, <u>more and more men and women</u> believed in the Lord and <u>were added to their number</u>.

- Acts 6:1 - In those days when <u>the number of disciples was increasing</u>...

- Acts 6:7 - So the word of God spread. The <u>number of disciples</u> in Jerusalem <u>increased rapidly</u>, and <u>a large number of priests</u> became obedient to the faith.

- Acts 9:31 - Then the church throughout Judea, Galilee and Samaria enjoyed a time of peace and was strengthened. Living in the fear of the Lord and encouraged by the Holy Spirit, <u>it increased in numbers</u>.

- Acts 9:42 - This became known all over Joppa, and <u>many people</u> believed in the Lord.

- Acts 11: 21 - The Lord's hand was with them, and <u>a great number of people</u> believed and turned to the Lord.

- Acts 11: 24 - He was a good man, full of the Holy Spirit and faith, and <u>a great number of people</u> were brought to the Lord.

- Acts 14:1 - There they spoke so effectively that <u>a great number of Jews and Greeks</u> believed.

- Acts 14:21 - They preached the Gospel in that city and <u>won a large number of disciples</u>.

- Acts 16:5 - So the churches were strengthened in the faith and <u>grew daily in numbers</u>.

- Acts 17:4 - <u>Some of the Jews</u> were persuaded and joined Paul and Silas, as did <u>a large number of God-fearing Greeks</u> and <u>quite a few prominent women</u>.

- Acts 17:12 - As a result, <u>many of them</u> believed, as did also <u>a number of prominent Greek women</u> and <u>many Greek men</u>.

- Acts 17:34 - <u>Some of the people</u> became followers of Paul and believed... and <u>a number of others</u>.

- Acts 18:8 - ...and <u>many of the Corinthians</u> who heard Paul believed and were baptized.

- Acts 19:5-7 - On hearing this, they were baptized in the name of the Lord Jesus... <u>there were about 12 men in all</u>.

Someone must have been counting! Numbers were obviously important to him or her.

Why do numbers matter? Because God has given us a mandate to reach *the entire world* with the Good News! We can't fulfill this mandate if our churches don't grow, unless we plant A LOT more churches. Certainly there are more people in your city, town or village that need a relationship with Christ. If not, you've fished out your pond and need to consider planting a church in another location. Remember: the light was made to shine in the darkness, not among other lights.

Numbers aren't the most important gauge of our effectiveness, but they do at least give us an idea of our footprint (our reach). As Ed Stetzer says, "Facts are our friends." Dr. Brooks taught me to count *everything* and *everyone*. He says that if you don't track trends you won't be able to stay ahead of the curve, and you'll often be taken by surprise. This is dangerous as a leader. If things are often taking you by surprise your people will lose confidence in your leadership.

As I said, we need a way to track our growth. We need to know how many people are in the service, the nursery, the Kids Church and the youth group. We need to know how many people are involved in small groups. We need to know this information in order to properly prepare for growth. Suppose your Kids Church starts to outgrow their facilities. How will you know how much space you need? You should have an idea of how much square footage it takes per child to minister to them properly and safely, and what is the most effective way to divide the Kids Church classes (age, gender, grade). You will also need to know how many parking spaces are needed in case you have to expand your facility.

Many people have a real problem with this, concluding that we only care about the numbers. But Pastor Perry Noble answers this argument beautifully. He says that if you count your offerings and not your people you are revealing what you really care about: money.

People matter deeply to God and to us. It is important that we know who is in our services so we can effectively pastor them. He has entrusted them into our care and we never want to take that lightly. This is why we count everything!

The Number That Really Counts

We recently assisted some friends with the launch of their church in Texas. When I spoke with the pastor a few weeks later he told me that it seemed everyone wanted to know how many people he had in the service, but no one asked how many people made commitments to Christ. It excited me to hear him say this. He gets the big picture! He realizes that we need to be reaching people that are far from God, not just growing big churches.

While we love seeing churches grow, the number of attenders doesn't tell the whole story. The number that really counts is how many people make decisions for Christ. We need to keep a close eye on the number of converts and baptisms in our churches. If we aren't seeing people regularly make decisions for Christ, we need to get on our face before God and ask Him how to change this! Why? Lost people matter to God! Jesus wants all people to be saved to know the truth.[116] He doesn't want anyone to be lost, but rather that all people would repent.[117] And He has invited us into the family business of introducing people to our Heavenly Father.

In Luke 15, Jesus gives us three parables that reveal God's heart for people that are far from Him. He concludes the first two parables with the following lines:

- *"In the same way, I tell you there is more joy in heaven over one sinner who changes his heart and life, than over ninety-nine good people who don't need to change."* (Verse 7 NCV)

- *"In the same way, there is joy in the presence of the angels of God when one sinner changes his heart and life."* (Verse 10 NCV)

And in the last one, the Parable of the Lost (Prodigal) Son, Jesus portrays God as a father who throws a huge feast when his lost son returns! If God is *this focused* on people that are far from Him and their salvation produces such incredible rejoicing in heaven, maybe we should make this a priority in our ministries as well.

Systems

Although I'm not going to take a lot of time to focus on creating effective systems, I feel the need to hit some high points. There are many great books and organizations that can help church leaders create systems that actually encourage innovation and growth. Andy Stanley often says, "Your system is perfectly designed to get the results you're getting." And he's right.

Some pastors will argue, "We don't have any systems." I disagree. Nearly every church has systems for greeting, volunteer training, Kids Church, worship or sound team involvement, visitor and altar care (prayer and follow-up), handling the offering, etc. Even something as simple as, "Talk with Pastor Brown if you have any questions" is a system. Many times church volunteer recruitment systems look more like, "We need more helpers in Kids Church. You can sign up at the Info Table to get involved." While this may make people aware of a need, it casts no vision for working with the kids in your church. You will probably only get "warm bodies" in response to this type of appeal.

"Heavy hitters" (high capacity leaders) typically won't answer such an appeal for help. They need to be invited *personally*. If your system involves:

- A pastor or Kids Church leader/volunteer personally asking them to check out a Kids Church service,

- Talking with them afterwards about what they saw, asking them for honest feedback,

- And then inviting them to impact the future by pouring biblical principles into the future civic and church leaders, innovators and change agents,

… you're more likely to get a positive response from someone that can help you take this ministry to the next level – especially if you offer them a trial period of three to six months so they don't feel they're stuck. In other words, your systems will either enable or hinder momentum. There is much more we could say about momentum, but that is another subject for another book.

Your systems also need to be scalable. The "Talk with Pastor Brown" system works in a Mom & Pop church, but will fail to be effective if the church grows to 400 people (a highly unlikely occurrence for a Mom & Pop church). It will wear Pastor Brown out and will frustrate the people. And ultimately, some details will fall through the cracks.

You need to think through how you can streamline the systems you have, making them more effective and preparing for growth. The farther down the line you can push decision-making and the creation and implementation of systems, the better. Of course you'll want to have some oversight of the process. But if you will give your volunteers a say in the ministries they are involved with, they will take more ownership in those ministries.

Discussion Questions:

What does a win look like for your setting?

What qualities do you look for when choosing a leader?

What are some creative ways you can cast vision to your people?

How are you doing quality control on the different aspects of your Sunday morning experience?

Who are the top 20% of people in your organization? What are some practical ways you can intentionally invest in them?

Who are you training to take the reins of the organization? How are you training them? What does your succession plan (timeline) look like?

What metrics do you use to track your effectiveness? Are you regularly studying them to discover patterns and opportunities?

ACTION

Getting Your Hands Dirty

As we've said, today's younger generations are desperate for their lives to make an impact. This is an area where the church can truly shine. Remember, we have been called to be the light of the world. When we go beyond the walls of our church to serve the hurting, the depressed, the devastated and the broken, God's true heart is revealed. We *have to* maintain a presence in our communities. And we need to invest in the international community as well. We do this through serving and outreach.

Although getting your hands dirty does include evangelism, we're not talking about going door-to-door or holding tent crusades. We're mainly talking about *practical ministry* to those in need. We are called to "speak up for those that cannot speak for themselves."[118] We're also talking about serving with no strings attached, just like Jesus did! The unchurched will serve alongside our church members if we're doing something that matters to them. Doing so expands the footprint of our churches, and it makes our churches attractive to young adults that want to make a difference.

Chapter 19
Going Beyond Your Church Walls

Any church that attracts unchurched young adults will necessarily have to maintain a presence in the local community and contribute to the international community. This happens only through the intentional investment of time, strategic planning, manpower and resources. Today's young people feel a responsibility to invest their time and gifts into helping those less fortunate, and to alleviate suffering throughout the world. Churches have to be about the business of helping people find avenues to make a positive impact on the world.

The first step is to get our people *out* of the church and *into* the world. We will have no impact in our community if we're not connecting with people in *their* world. When our people go beyond our church's walls and start making an impact in their world, the natural connection to our church will eventually come. But it won't happen if our outreaches are simply a means to this end. If we only do outreaches for the sake of growing our churches they will ultimately prove fruitless.

One of the things that we discover in the Book of Acts is that the Early Church found a rhythm that positioned them for growth. As I've already pointed out, the believers gathered for encouragement and empowerment and then scattered for impact. Through this model they were able to both bring people far from God into a relationship with Him and to disciple the new converts.

Social Justice

As we mentioned before, one of the biggest buzzwords in today's culture is social justice. This simply means doing everything within our power to right the wrongs in our world, whether it's modern-day slavery, poverty, lack of access to food or clean water, bullying or a myriad of other issues. God has placed us here to represent Him and His heart, which means we are to be a force for good in this world. Rather than only thinking about ourselves or those we love, we need to take up the plight of those that are suffering and neglected, those that have no voice.

"I don't preach a social gospel; I preach the gospel, period. The gospel of our Lord Jesus Christ is concerned for the whole person. When people were hungry, Jesus didn't say, 'Now is that political or social?' He said, 'I feed you.' Because the good news to a hungry person is bread."

Desmond Tutu

Millennials and the generations that follow aren't satisfied to just send finances; they want to personally GO and BE a change agent! There are so many inequities and wrongs in the world that the Church is uniquely qualified to make right. Issues such a human trafficking, poverty and lack of access to sanitary food, drink and living conditions need to be addressed. Social justice is simply a phrase used to describe the process of making the world a better place. At times this term is used to justify greed by "taking what I am owed from those that don't deserve it." But it can also signify believers taking their place as God's hands and feet in this earth. We must feed the correct definition.

It is important for churches to offer opportunities to serve the underprivileged, the desperate and the despairing. Many of our people want to do something but don't know where to start. We've found it most effective when serving starts at the grassroots level, such as in a small group. Your groups can each find a place to serve – say, a food shelter. Then they can continue to serve on a monthly or quarterly basis. It gives us a larger footprint in the community and gets our people into the habit of serving regularly. If serving becomes a habit, our people will be more prepared to recognize and take advantage of opportunities to serve as they come.

A church-wide serving project can also be quite effective. It enables us to bring a lot of focus, manpower and resources to bear on a single problem. We've seen churches collect tens of thousands of shoes for African kids, raise large amounts of money to dig clean water wells for villages in developing countries and raise awareness of the plight of modern day sex slaves found in developed countries. They have the biggest impact on our churches when we send teams, not just money, to help. It brings a personal connection when we hear a team's stories afterwards. These outreaches and mission trips can have an even bigger impact if we join forces with other churches or organizations that are already elbow deep in the fray. Why would we try to reinvent the wheel?

Having said that, we can't afford to send our people on international sightseeing trips where they paint a few buildings under the guise of a "mission trip." Mission trips need to turn a person's world upside down. When done correctly, they will impact the ones being sent more than the ones to whom they are sent. Going on a mission trip should be a disorienting experience, whether in your own city or overseas. This is why it's so important to debrief an experience with the mission team before they return to the real world.

Over the centuries the Church has lost her voice because her believers have hidden within the confines of their local church buildings. It's time that we go outside the walls of our churches and be the change agents we were created to be. We were created in the image of God.[119]   God influences His environment (everything!). In the same way, we were created to have an impact on ours.

The Little Village Idol
In 1999, I took a team of college students to the village of Xaltepec, in Puebla, Mexico for a mission trip to plant a church. As the local pastor gave me a tour of the village he showed me

the Catholic Church. I grew up Catholic, so I am quite used to the statues, shrines and icons. But near the altar I saw something that disturbed me. Next to the statues of Jesus, Joseph and Mary was the image of an Aztec god (a sun disk with an angry looking face).

When I asked about it the pastor told me, "This is the local village idol. The villagers believe it is very powerful here, although it has no power outside the village." At that point I felt God speaking in my heart. He said, "Too many Christians treat me like a local village idol. They believe I have a lot of power within the walls of their church, but very little on the outside." If what we have doesn't work outside of the walls of a church, then we don't have anything to offer. We can't afford to act this way. We're robbing the world of the knowledge of God's grace and mercy!

The God of the universe is waiting for us to take our place as change agents in this world! His power knows no end. He lives in us and is waiting for us to cooperate with Him to bring His will to pass!

In the ministry of Jesus as recorded in the Bible we discover Him meeting needs on a very practical level. He brought healing to the sick, the blind, the deaf and the mute, as well as to the lepers. He also healed the mentally disturbed, delivered the demon possessed, fed the multitudes and raised the dead. All of these are very *practical* ways of serving people. He met their needs. Each miracle brought God praise and gave Jesus a platform to speak into peoples' lives.

Every time believers serve they earn a voice in the community, especially if they serve on a continual basis. But we have to serve with a humble attitude, not in a condescending manner. We must come as servants, not as philanthropists helping the poor miserable wretches of the earth. When we serve with a humble spirit it attracts the attention of a world that is far from God. Why? Most people serve for selfish reasons – to pad their résumé, get a photo op or to build their self-esteem. We should serve out of gratitude for what God has done for us.

We've already written about how our church got a positive brand in the city of Freiburg. We did it by serving. We didn't wait for opportunities; we created them. We looked for ways to serve our community... and we found them. We did free grill parties, Easter Egg Hunts, "Oprah's Big Give"-style outreaches, adopt-a-school and free flea markets, in addition to serving the hungry/homeless and helping raise money for impoverished children in a citywide initiative.

We asked God to show us needs in our own neighborhood. Then we walked the streets and prayed, and prayed, and prayed. As we spoke with our church's neighbors and community leaders, a few common themes came to light. We asked our team to help us think through how we could meet those needs. We acted in response to a belief that God had situated us in that area to meet the needs of our community. And *He* provided the resources for us to do it.

Here in the USA many churches are doing the same thing. They look for needs in their communities and seek out creative ways to meet them. They volunteer to setup and clean up for civic events (parades, fireworks displays, etc.), they bring breakfast or snacks to fire/police departments and emergency rooms, they provide free marriage and parenting classes, they offer 12-step programs for addicts, they do free after-school tutoring, they offer a day of pampering and free car repairs for single mothers and assist food kitchens or homeless shelters in ministering to the less fortunate.

Such things are a perfect representation of the heart of God. And they are remarkably attractive to the unchurched Millennials we so desperately want to reach. Many times people that are not a part of our churches will volunteer to help us with community outreaches if we'll just get the word out. As they do so, they form relationships with our church people, allowing them to see what believers are like in the real world.

A final thought on this point (we've already made this point but it bears repeating): If pastors don't model engagement with the community around them, their people won't either. I know it's not "safe." I'm a very social person, but I still like the safety of an established relationship where I know what to expect and I don't have to make myself vulnerable.

But I also know that if I want my people to go outside of their comfort zone and engage a broken world that doesn't even know it's lost, I have to do it first. As John Maxwell says, "Everything rises and falls on leadership." Maybe you have to pray for courage. Maybe you have to ask God to show you the "lost" through Jesus' eyes. Do whatever it takes. Nothing will change until the leadership – especially the pastor – changes, and takes up the vision as their own. We need to be willing to get outside of OUR comfort zone before we ask our people to do so. If pastors don't, their people won't!

Chapter 20
Sharing Your Faith With The Unchurched

This concept of getting our hands dirty also includes sharing our faith with people far from God. Why, then do we have such a hard time with evangelism? One reason is that we believe that people just aren't interested. But that's often not the case at all.

Thom Rainer wrote an interesting blog post entitled *Seven Common Comments Non-Christians Make About Christians.* Among the surprising points (and corresponding comments) brought up by non-Christians in a survey were:

- I would like to develop a friendship with a Christian. "I'm really interested in what they believe and how they carry out their beliefs. I wish I could find a Christian that would be willing to spend some time with me."

- I would like to learn about the Bible from a Christian. "The Bible really fascinates me, but I don't want to go to a stuffy and legalistic church to learn about it. It would be nice if a Christian invited me to study the Bible in his home or at a place like Starbucks."

- I wish I could learn to be a better husband, wife, dad, mom, etc., from a Christian. "My wife is threatening to divorce me, and I think she means it this time. My neighbor is a Christian, and he seems to have it together. I am swallowing my pride and asking him to help me."

- I wish a Christian would take me to his or her church. "I really would like to visit a church, but I'm not particularly comfortable going by myself. *What is weird is that I am 32 years old, and I've never had a Christian invite me to church in my entire life.*"[120] [emphasis mine]

The unchurched would love to hear more about God and the Bible from someone with experience. They are sometimes even willing to check out our churches. But starting that conversation is so awkward for believers that it often never happens.

Coffee Evangelism

Christ-followers in the trenches, living and working in the real, everyday world really *can* make a difference in the life of a person that is far from God. But most believers don't realize this. They've rarely, if ever, been told that they can. We've instead heard stories of superstars that win hundreds, if not thousands, of people to Christ. They make it sound so easy that the rest of us feel like losers.

We've got to get beyond our insecurities and out of our comfort zone. We spend so much time and energy in our churches trying to lure people *into* our buildings when we should instead be going out to where *they already are*. The most effective place to share our faith *isn't* in our churches; it's in the lunchroom or the next cubicle, on the basketball court or in the next driveway.

The longer we wait, the more intimidating it becomes. The only way to overcome our fear of sharing our faith is simply to jump in. We taught our Watermarkers to pray for opportunities, look for opportunities and then take advantage of those opportunities.

I think another reason we have a hard time reaching the unreached is that Christians often answer questions the unchurched just aren't asking. Or when faced with an honest question they simply repeat the apologetic answers they've been taught. There's no life or conviction in the "prepared statements" we learn in most church evangelism programs.

175

Jesus was EXTREMELY popular with "outsiders" because His words brought grace and life. If you'll study His interactions with people, you'll see that He really listened to people when they spoke to Him. And He responded authentically and honestly. This opened their hearts to what He had to say.

When I was a teenager a popular church evangelism program taught us how to lead a person to Christ by asking questions. The problem was that we were taught to ask leading questions designed to back a person into a corner with his or her answers. The only logical outcome was for the person to commit his or her life to Jesus. This never worked for me! Why? It wasn't real. It didn't come from my heart. It wasn't a conversation that flowed from a genuine relationship with the person.

The solution is to have a real conversation, getting to know a person. It's not about arguing beliefs or proving that my way is right. I have to first *earn* the right to speak into a person's life. As my friend, Steve Muscarella, says, "If you want to lead a person to Christ, you have to first drink a cup of coffee with him/her." Actually, it will take more than just one cup of coffee in today's increasingly cynical postmodern world!

Years ago I was asked to train and lead a youth group from southeastern Germany in street evangelism. This definitely isn't my favorite thing to do because it's not really my style. But I wanted to support my friend, the youth pastor of this group.

I taught the group how to approach someone and begin a conversation. I focused on how to really connect with a person instead of just preaching to/at him or her. I shared how to read a person's body language and look for opportunities. And I finished with, "It's *entirely okay* not to push them to give their heart to Jesus if you sense that they aren't willing or ready. But do ask them if you can pray with them." Then we all prayed together.

His youth group and I went downtown and split up. I found a young man on a bench drinking a beer and watching the skateboarders do their thing. I said hi and introduced myself as an American youth worker trying to get to know the local youth culture. He invited me to sit down by him. We talked about his town, his family and his school. He even opened up about his hopes and dreams.

All of a sudden a spiritual conversation just happened. I didn't force it at all. God was at work! This young man shared about his relatives that were religious, although they didn't really live what they said they believed. He said he wished there was a God but just had a hard time believing in something he couldn't see.

The opportunity came for me to share my story when my friend, the youth pastor, walked up. Not wanting to be rude, I introduced him to this young man. My friend proceeded to hijack the conversation and started preaching hellfire and brimstone to this guy. I wanted to cuss; I really did! But my friend was on a roll, and he kept on going. Eventually the guy had heard enough and said, "I've gotta go."

As he walked away, my friend said, "I guess I was just casting pearls before swine." I wanted to punch him right in the face... er... I mean, pray for him! He screwed up a God-given opportunity! I had EARNED the right to share *my* story by listening to this young man's story. And my friend butted in and blew it!

As I tried to explain to my friend what went wrong I could see I was wasting my words. He just didn't get it. I wondered if *I* was the one casting pearls before swine.

You have to be willing to *really listen* to a person's point of view and actually *validate* his or her viewpoint, even if you don't agree with it. They are just as entitled to their worldview as I am to mine. It doesn't have to make sense to me in order for me to validate their right to believe as they see fit.

Please understand that I'm not watering down the fact that Jesus is the one and only way into a relationship with God. I am simply trying to help people realize that the days of "turn or burn" are long gone. While radical statements like these may work for some, most are turned off entirely. If you aren't willing to invest in a real relationship with an unchurched person, she often isn't willing to give up her precious time to hear what you have to say.

In the pluralism of Post-Christian culture it is entirely plausible for a person to affirm two beliefs that are polar opposites at the same time. Today's younger generations have no problem believing that life begins at conception, but also affirming a woman's right to choose whether or not to abort the child. This problem will also lead to some very interesting (read: frustrating) counseling sessions. We have some wild stories we could share, but we want to protect people's privacy.

This is where apologetics is actually quite helpful. Apologetics, in the context of Christianity, deals with the defense of our faith in God. I was taught to use apologetic arguments to destroy any opposition to faith in Christ. But this style of evangelism just doesn't work anymore.

But I have found that the apologetic reasoning I learned is very palatable to unchurched people when I use it to gently challenge a person's wrong beliefs about God or Christianity. When it comes across more like a question or a suggestion, people are open to it: "If what you say is true, then what about _____?" or, "Have you considered _____?" These aren't confrontational, but instead an invitation to have a deeper conversation. The answers the person gives have the added benefit of helping us understand his/her world.

You also have to be comfortable with unanswered questions. Unchurched people ask questions that are "off limits" in normal churches. Churched people know where the boundaries are, and they have been taught to stay far away. But unlike longtime churchgoers, unchurched people are curious. If they feel they are only getting a rehearsed stock answer to their questions, or if they feel they will get shut down when asking, you will lose your chance to connect with them. It's absolutely okay to say, "I don't know. Let me research that and get back with you." Or better yet, "What do *you* think?"

To be honest, we Christ-followers don't like to do this. It takes too much of an investment. It requires too much of our time and energy. And it gets quite messy when you deal with the real problems in people's lives.

We've forgotten that Jesus called us to make DISCIPLES not converts. The discipleship process is up-close and personal. It is a struggle. Daily in-the-trenches work always is. We want the exciting flash-bang of instant results. But real life doesn't work that way. Besides, God is more interested in the process than in the event.

One more thought about evangelism: Just as we must learn to do church in a vacuum, we also need to learn to share our faith in a vacuum, making absolutely no assumptions. We can't just quote Bible verses and expect the unchurched to agree with them or believe them. Don't assume they have a biblical background. We have to be prepared to share the Gospel with someone that doesn't believe the Bible is God's Word. The best way to do this is for us to share our story, what God has done for us. We can practice it beforehand, but when sharing it, we must speak authentically in order to capture their hearts.

A Missionary To Your Neighborhood

A friend told us her pastor gave the following illustration: Imagine a tic-tac-toe board in which your house is the middle square. Now write in the names of your neighbors in the surrounding houses (squares on the game board). Begin praying that God would send someone to your neighbors; and while you're at it, ask Him to send YOU.

If you don't know your neighbors, you can start there! Take the time and energy to get to know your neighbors instead of closing your garage door as fast as you can to avoid uncomfortable conversations. When you both are outside at the same time you could ask a question or two about their life/job/family, or maybe give them a compliment on their house, car or yard. Or if you want to really be adventurous, invite them over for dinner. The important thing is to start where you are rather than waiting for some big opportunity. If you don't take advantage of small opportunities the big ones never seem to come.

I like to initiate a conversation with the cashier at the store and see where it leads. At a restaurant you could engage your server in conversation (and actually LISTEN) before leaving a *big* tip. At dinner recently Robin got the opportunity to invite our server to church simply because we started a conversation with him. He seemed excited that a customer would invite him to church.

Let me be honest with you: Some of my efforts in this area aren't very successful. Sometimes they are downright ugly. But isn't that life? I'm not successful every time I try to share my faith. But each time I try something and then learn from my mistakes I get better at it. Just because it doesn't work one time doesn't mean I will utterly fail every time. We have a job to do! Jesus is coming back soon and I want to take as many people as possible with me to heaven.

People Of Peace

Jesus told his disciples to look for "people of peace."[121] These are people that God has prepared to receive the message. But it doesn't stop there. People of peace will bring their circle of influence to you. It's a way to multiply your influence among the unchurched. If you can connect with them they will open up their world to you. You need to earnestly pray for people of peace to cross your path, and that you'll connect with them. Finding a person of peace opens God-sized doors!

Strangely enough people of peace aren't always who you'd expect. For Jesus it was a Samaritan woman with a sordid past.[122] As I mentioned before, in the eyes of most devout Rabbis of Jesus' day she had three strikes against her – She was a Samaritan, a woman and had a very checkered past. But because Jesus was willing to speak to her with love and respect – even as He challenged her prejudices – she brought the entire city to Him.

Barnabas was also a person of peace. When he heard that Saul (Paul) had become a believer he went to find him. Until his conversion Saul had been going from town to town arresting believers and applauding as they were tortured and martyred. He was both hated and feared by the believers.

After connecting with Paul, Barnabas used his credibility and influence with the Christians to bring Paul into their circle. Through this connection the footprint of the Gospel grew rapidly!

For us it was the Director of a Freiburg grade school that had a large percentage of poor Muslim immigrant students. Our family chose to take most of the money we would normally use for Christmas presents and instead buy supplies and clothes for at-risk kids in this man's school. He was very cautious at first, thinking we were going to try to evangelize his school. But because we did it with such a positive attitude and didn't try to use this as an evangelistic outreach he said he would be open to our church helping them with some projects. But it was still, "Don't call us; we'll call you."

Shortly thereafter our church did a "Servolution"[123] outreach to the city. Robin and I gave our church family envelopes with cash in them (from our personal savings) and asked them to find a way to multiply it and use it to serve the city with no strings attached. The only rules were that they couldn't spend it on themselves or their friends, and they had to document what they did with the money. We asked them to take pictures or video footage of their Servolution, if possible.

Some of our people adopted this same school (on their own initiative), bringing breakfast to the teachers and staff, and presents for the kids. As a result the Director invited our church to help repair their playground teepees. And then we got to paint the teepees alongside some of the first and second graders. We even got positive press coverage and a mention on their school website, which is virtually unheard of in secular Germany! Connecting with your person of peace will give you credibility and influence in your community.

Discussion Questions:

What are the greatest needs in your community? How can you discover what the needs of your community are? How can you meet these needs in a practical way?

What do you think about Jon's statement that we need to learn to share our faith in a vacuum?

How would you tell someone about Jesus and His love if you couldn't quote the Bible? How could you spark someone's interest in Jesus if they had never heard of or know very little about Christianity?

What are some practical ways to develop a culture of serving in your church?

What are some practical ways to get out of your Christian bubble and engage with unchurched people?

How do you recognize a person of peace? Is there anyone that fits this description within your circle of relationships?

AVAILABILITY

Family Matters

Genuine community is a hallmark of true Christ followers. The Early Church experienced explosive growth because the believers did life together![124]

Our world is more digitally connected than ever. But at the same time there is less face-to-face interaction than at any time in history. This is a problem because we were created to be in relationship with one another.[125] Unchurched people sense something is missing, even if they can't put their finger on what it is. The church is uniquely qualified to fill this void!

Chapter 21
True Community

On one of the first pages of our Bibles we discover God saying, "It's not good for man to be alone."[126] He created us to be *inter*connected and *inter*dependent. Relationships were *His* idea.

In Western society we pride ourselves on our technological advances. We have not only landed men on the moon; we are now preparing to do the same on Mars. We can even "print" human replacement parts! In the 1960s Stanley Milgram concluded through his experiment that there are only six degrees of separation between any two people on the planet. I believe this is shrinking rapidly because of the Internet and social media. But along with the benefits of technology there are also burdens.

We are more digitally connected than ever. We can connect with our friends and family across town and throughout the globe through email, text, chat, Facebook, Twitter, Skype or a myriad of other social media and messaging platforms. We provide real-time updates for our online "tribe" – our community – some of whom we've never even met. But at the same time we're becoming more relationally detached. Today we have less face-to-face interaction than at any time in human history.

As our world becomes more relationally disengaged, our need for genuine community grows exponentially. In our goal to achieve interconnectedness through the Internet and social media we have actually produced a society that is growing further apart. People are hungry for real-life connection points, though they may not know how to verbalize it. Today it is much easier to go online and pretend to be someone you're not than to actually do the hard work of developing face-to-face relationships.

This is the perfect "hole" for churches to fill. Churches are natural gathering places, offering multiple connection points and face-to-face interaction. We have to be intentional about making our churches *even more* relational, especially as they grow larger. True biblical community never happens by accident. It must begin with the pastor and leaders. They will have to lead their people into what they want to see.

Let me add that there *is* a need for online ministry. Many Millennials will watch a service online to determine if they even want to visit the church. Others prefer the anonymity that an online congregation offers. Some like the style of ministry in a church that is far away. Offering an online experience allows them to connect with God through your services. And it provides a way for your people that are traveling to stay connected to your church. *We can't afford to dismiss this important area of ministry for our churches.*

Having said that, let's focus on the relational aspect of our churches. I read an interesting article about a large atheist church in London. It contained a note-worthy sentence:

> *But the Sunday Assembly's success — 400 Londoners packed into last week's two services, while 60 had to be turned away at the door — suggests many urban atheists crave the sense of community that comes with joining a church.*[127]

This atheist church has figured something out that many Christian churches have forgotten: **we were created for community.**

So much time and effort goes into making our churches high tech, high energy, produced and polished. But what the culture around us is begging for is true connection. Reggie Joiner often says, "The church will never be able to out-Disney Disney." And that's true, we will never have the budget or resources to be the most entertaining or engaging environment on the planet. But even if we did… what would be the point?

While we can't out-Disney Disney, no one should be able to out-community the local church.[128]

Although bells and whistles used to be effective in reaching young people, today the church "market" is oversaturated with these things. "Cool church" isn't all that cool anymore. Bells and whistles just aren't that important to a media-driven audience. Millennials would rather have *authentic* churches that are filled with *genuine* people where they can find *real* relationships.

Among Jesus' final words to His disciples were,

> *"Love one another. In the same way I have loved you, you love one another. This is how everyone will recognize that you are my disciples – when they see the love you have for each other."[129]*

He then prayed that His disciples would be unified in the same way that He and the Father are. In this prayer we see His desire for unity, interconnectedness and interdependence among His followers! And notice the end result of this community: the world will take notice! This is one of the most underestimated ways to show a messed up world – the world outside our church walls – that the Jesus we talk about inside our church walls is alive and well.

The Proper Environment For Growth

It is within an interconnected group of people that real life change happens. Think about it... we can "fake it" with our church friends, classmates and coworkers. But our family and our roommates get to know the *real* us. In this setting our faith is tested and our true colors are displayed. It is easy to "act" like a Christian with people I only see a couple of hours per week in a social setting. But the down and dirty, everyday hard work of interconnected relationships forces us to come to grips with who we really are.

Jesus likened His relationship with His followers to that of a vine and its branches. The branches draw the nourishing sap from the vine and produce fruit. Jesus told His disciples, "If you remain in me and I in you, you will bear much fruit. Apart from me you can do nothing."[130]

The Apostle Paul explains what this "fruit" looks like in the real world. He provides his readers with a list of character traits that are to spring out of our relationship with God.

> *But the fruit of the Spirit is love, joy, peace, forbearance, kindness, goodness, faithfulness, gentleness and self-control. Against such things there is no law.*

Galatians 5:22-23

Growing up, I thought that the only way to grow spiritually was to spend time alone with God. Don't get me wrong - this *is* extremely important! Solitude is a spiritual discipline that positions me to hear the voice of God more clearly.[131]

But if we look at the list of spiritual fruit Paul gave us, it's easy to see that these fruits are best developed within the context of community. I don't need patience, kindness, goodness or gentleness in my "prayer closet." I need them when I interact with others. It's easy to "walk in love"[132] with people I only see once a week. But when I am truly connected with other human beings I am forced to adjust so that we can develop/maintain a relationship. It is in this context that I learn that the world doesn't revolve around me.

I believe Paul intentionally used fruit as a metaphor because of its sweetness when fully ripe. It nourishes the body while delighting the taste buds. But fruit that is not fully formed or ripe is sour and sometimes even unpalatable. Because many believers are not engaged in biblical community the fruit they produce is often small and sour, at best.

I recently heard a pastor discussing spiritual growth. He recounted a time when his wife made a loaf of bread dough and put it into the freezer until they were ready to bake it. He explained that even though all the ingredients were mixed in, the yeast wasn't activated until the dough was placed in the right environment. He brought the dough to work with him and placed it in front of a space heater. In a matter of minutes the dough began to grow exponentially. Why? It was in the right environment to activate the yeast.[133]

Genuine community provides the proper environmental variables for the fruit of the spirit to be produced in our lives. It is where true discipleship takes place. Both positive and negative experiences are necessary in order for me to experience healthy spiritual growth. Actually, negative experiences are a lot like "organic fertilizer" (the kind that comes from the backside of a cow) – at least that's what it feels like. This type of fertilizer is necessary for fruits like patience and self-control to be fully developed.

Bless Them When They Come. Bless Them When They Go.

Church planters, you need to realize that most of the people that help you start a church won't be with you in a year. Just prepare for it now. This is no excuse to avoid developing deep relationships with your team. If you aren't relationally connected you won't be able to build a church that is.

We lost two Russian families from our Launch Team a week after we started because they disagreed with our Halloween Outreach. Through this outreach we saw five kids come to Christ! Two more families from our team left after a year, which was the commitment I had asked them for. But most of our Launch Team members remained with us until we had to make a hard decision about choosing another meeting location. We knew there would be pushback, but we had no idea how ingrained the German culture is when it comes to congregational voting on issues. Our church government wasn't set up this way, and it upset some of our core team members. We lost more team members when my family had to return to the US for a while to help our extended family.

Because we focused so much on doing life together, we decided to "bless them when they come and bless them when they go."[134] If we had held onto our people with tightly closed fists, they would have resented us. Many of the ones that left ended up in other good churches in town because of the way we handled things. A few actually came back.

If they leave your church with baggage and then don't like the next church, they're more likely to leave that church and never come back – becoming a "done." But if they leave with your blessing, the door is open for them to return if they discover they've made the wrong decision.

We knew that our church was not the right church for every person or family. There were some other great churches in our area where people who were dissatisfied with our church could grow and get involved. If someone wasn't happy at Watermark, we wanted him or her to find a church where they *could* be happy. It wouldn't have helped at all for us to hold onto people just to pad our numbers, or for loyalty's sake. This comes from a heart that cares about them as a person, not just for what they do for our church.

Can I insert this "aside?" If you have an issue with your pastor, please ask yourself some questions:

- Is this issue something that affects my relationship with God?

- Is it something that decreases my trust in him/her as my pastor?

These are both *substance* issues. If the answer to either question is yes, you may need to prayerfully consider finding another church where you *can* hook up and get involved. Find a church whose vision matches what is in your heart. While you'll never find a *perfect* church, it's probably healthier for you *and* for your current church if you just move on.

You aren't going to change your church leadership! Find a church where you can get involved and throw yourself into serving. There is so much work to be done for the Kingdom of God that we can't afford to waste time fighting.

On the other hand, sometimes in this type of situation the best thing for us to do is to remain at our post. Many times our frustrations are simply differences of *style*, not *substance*. In such cases, to cut and run would stunt our growth spiritually. A muscle can't grow unless it first undergoes stress and strain. It's the same way with our faith. Oftentimes God will use these differences to bring us to a place of deeper reliance on Him, strengthening our faith.

If you do decide to stay, throw your heart into serving. Support the leadership with a humble heart. Be your pastor's greatest cheerleader. Pray for him/her. Remember that leading a church isn't easy. It's often quite ugly. He/she needs your prayers, as does his/her family.

People Versus Tasks

What good is it for us to get everything on our 'To Do List' accomplished, but fail to connect with and minister to the precious people God sends us?

Paraphrase of Mark 8:36

God spoke to us *very clearly* even before we started Watermark that one of our mantras was to be, "It's all about the journey!" – that relationships were to always trump accomplishing a task. We were never to allow ourselves to be too busy to connect with people. Often in churches we get so myopic in preparing for a service that we become overwhelmed with all the things that have to be done – everything from making sure the media elements of our message are finished to making sure the stage looks right, etc. We get so caught up in the *doing* that we forget about the *being*. We are called to *be* servants and to represent God's heart toward people.

We can't afford to miss the entire point of a church service. It's a *communal* celebration of the goodness and grace of God. Pastors naturally tend to focus on the God factor, but often forget the community factor. If we neglect the God factor, we merely have a social club. If we disregard the community factor our people may have a spiritual experience, but they leave without the relational connection that God desires us to have. We miss out on a key element of what churches have to offer. It is the relational aspect of a church that makes people want to return, or as Pastor Larry Osborn says, it makes your church "sticky." To borrow a line from the 80's sitcom *Cheers*, a church needs to be a place "where everybody knows your name."

We mentioned before that we required our team to have all their pre-service preparation totally finished *one hour before* the service started. That way we could have team hangout time, a pre-service team meeting and prayer, and then be ready to receive the guests that God would send us. We encouraged our team members on Sunday to work on building deep relationships with each other, but when visitors arrived, it was all about them. Once the church people left the team hung out again for a long time. Sometimes my family didn't get back home until almost dinner time! The most important thing for us was doing life together.

Creating churches that are strong in biblical community is hard work. Trust me, we know! But the prize is well worth the price. It will not only create the proper environment for discipleship to take place; it will also affect the community around us. In a Post-Christian world places of true community will be lights in a dark world!

Chapter 22
Biblical Small Groups

In Acts 2 we find an account of something that occurred seven weeks after Jesus' death, burial and resurrection. We find 120 men and women gathered together in an upper room, united in prayer and waiting in obedience to Jesus for what He had promised them. Suddenly they were all filled with the Holy Spirit, which drew a large crowd. And as a result of the Apostle Peter's sermon to this crowd 3,000 people were added to the fledgling Church. Talk about church growth!!!

How do you disciple 3,000 new believers with a "staff" of only 120 people, most of whom are only volunteers? Thankfully Luke, author of the Book of Acts, was taking good notes. He records the following:

> *They devoted themselves to the apostles' teaching and to fellowship, to the breaking of bread and to prayer. Everyone was filled with awe at the many wonders and signs performed by the apostles. All the believers were together and had everything in common. They sold property and possessions to give to anyone who had need. Every day they continued to meet together in the temple courts. They broke bread in their homes and ate together with glad and sincere hearts, praising God and enjoying the favor of all the people. And the Lord added to their number daily those who were being saved.*

> *Acts 2:42-47*

They **devoted themselves** to a few things:

- Learning together

- Hanging out together

- Eating together

- Praying together

They shared their goods to meet each other's needs. They met together in the Temple courts every day and ate together in each other's homes. In other words, we could say that they truly did life together. This method of discipleship and community was extremely effective back then. It is just as effective today! The end result was that they developed a positive "brand" in their community, and that the Church grew daily.

Notice that one of the things mentioned in this account was that they ate together in each other's homes. This is a true picture of what small group ministry *can* be. In biblical small groups we know and are known. We are accepted for who we really are, not for the image we wish to project. And eating together brings the added benefit of setting people at ease, making them feel both welcomed and safe.

Unfortunately many churches offer small group programs that never go beyond surface level relationships. The groups gather to discuss the Bible and pray, but nothing deeper. While this isn't all bad, it's not the biblical definition of community. Notice that in the biblical account they truly did life together. There were no masks and no programs. From the information we're given it appears that these small groups were organic, formed by groups of believers that simply wanted to connect for mutual support and encouragement. As they did, the dynamic Jesus had developed with His disciples carried over to the entire Church.

Many churches, however, settle for a watered down version of small groups that merely connects people on a surface level. The leaders are taught how to lead a small group curriculum and to pray for their people. They are even prepared for problems that may occur. But not many of these leaders are ever really trained to move the group to a deeper relational level.

I believe this is because most pastors haven't personally grasped the value of community. It may be something they encourage their church members to be involved with, but *they* aren't involved a small group. *They* don't have a place to know and be known. They don't have a safe place to process the joys and struggles of life.

As I said before, we have to figure out how to make our churches smaller even while they are growing larger. The best way we've found is to get people involved in small groups. Small group leaders need to be trained to create a safe place for people to process what following Jesus looks like in the real world. Small groups that create this environment become incubators for people to take next steps in their faith.

Small groups can take many forms. Some meet weekly; others bi-monthly. The important thing is that they meet regularly. Some are affinity groups, gathering around activities that they love. Others are Bible studies, learning from the Bible and each other. Still others are topical, covering themes like parenting, money management and marriage. The most important thing is that each one becomes a safe place to process the joys and struggles of life.

Pastors also need to prepare their people for what to expect. Even though we want each group to do life together, the groups won't start out like this. Deep community is developed through time, consistency, intentionality and shared experience. People need to know that the more you invest in your small group and the more vulnerable you make yourself, the more you will get out of it.

When I was a teenager, my small group leader wasn't the coolest guy in the world. As a matter of fact, he was quite nerdy (a fact he readily admitted). But he truly loved us and did his best to make our group a place where we could know and be known. I must admit, the activities we did that required us to share our struggles and fears made me very uncomfortable. I didn't want to lay my life out in front of others. But as we prayed and played together I began to realize the value of this exercise. One of the guys from that group is among my best friends even today.

As we mentioned in the chapters on Alignment, the leader sets the tone for the entire group. If the leader is guarded in what he shares, his people will be as well. But if he instead opens up and makes himself vulnerable, he sets the example that the group will follow. By doing so he creates an environment of openness. And his group will be positioned to become a place where life change takes place.

As we open up our lives, we close the space between our group members and us. This encourages them to take a step towards us and toward each other. And we develop the true community the Bible talks about.

Jesus' Small Group

I believe Jesus understood this. That's why He intentionally chose an eclectic group of men to be His disciples. Don't believe me? Let's take a look at them. They were truly an interesting mix.

Let's start with Matthew... he was a tax collector, or we could say, a Roman collaborator. This is important to note because Israel was under Roman occupation. Tax collectors were truly a hated bunch. Actually, the Jewish people considered them to be an especially wicked class of "sinners."[135] They were working with the Romans to take a large percentage of the peoples' income as taxes, often demanding an extra amount on top of it. Tax collectors were the mobsters of their day and this was their version of "protection money."

Then you had Simon. No, not Simon Peter... we'll get to him later. I'm talking about Simon the Zealot. The Zealots were freedom fighters, doing everything possible – including guerrilla hit and run tactics – to free themselves from Roman rule. In their opinion the only good Roman was a dead Roman. And that included all that collaborated with the Romans. I'm sure there were some interesting political discussions between Matthew and him as they walked along the road.

And across the table from them sat the four fishermen, Peter and Andrew, James and John. They all worked for John's father, Zebedee. So even Peter and Andrew weren't of the same social class as James and John. Maybe this is why James and John's mom asked Jesus to give them special places of authority in His kingdom.[136]

Next we come to Thomas. He was the analytical one. He had a hard time believing that Jesus had actually risen from the dead. He demanded proof.

And finally, there was Judas. He was a schemer, a real ladder climber. The Apostle John tells us that he was appointed treasurer, and helped himself to what was in the moneybag. It's no wonder he was the one that betrayed Jesus.

Can you imagine the dynamic of this small group? It wasn't quite the bar scene from Star Wars, but it was approaching that.[137] No one in their right mind would pick such a diverse group to start a movement. But Jesus saw things differently than we do. He knew that our differences force us to come to grips with our insecurities and weaknesses. These provide the environment for us to grow.

Another benefit of small group ministry is the accountability that it brings. While we may pretend to be super-Christians at church on Sunday, a good small group will encourage us to let our guard down and be vulnerable. Someone that meets with us weekly and listens to our hurts, fears and struggles can help us take actual steps toward spiritual growth. They can strengthen us when we're weak, encourage us when we've failed and challenge us when we're tempted to do the wrong thing. They can also stand with us in prayer and rejoice with us when those prayers are answered.

Together Jesus' disciples worked through jealousy,[138] anger,[139] pride,[140] sorrow,[141] fear,[142] doubt[143] and joy.[144] In making themselves vulnerable to Jesus and to one another they positioned themselves to go to the next level spiritually.

Jesus took this same ragtag group of disciples and turned them into a spiritual force to be reckoned with. Because they learned to do life together as they followed Jesus, the Church was born. I am a Christ follower today because of their willingness to work together two millennia ago.

Discussion Questions:

What opportunities does our digitally connected, but relationally disengaged culture offer to the church?

Why are small groups so important to the discipleship process?

How can we be more vulnerable in our small groups?

Are you involved in a small group? If not, who are you doing life with? How can you make your small group more relational?

How can you emphasize the community factor in your church?

SECTION 3
It's Time To Engage!

Chapter 23
Where The Rubber Meets The Road

I've written a lot about the coming changes, and talked about how we dealt with them in Europe. I also tried to provide some suggestions for what it could look like in your setting. The questions at the end of each section can create some healthy discussion among your team about these topics and help you think through the process for your church.

But before I conclude this book, I want to leave you with some thoughts on how to implement what I've written.

For Pastors And Senior Leaders
Take the necessary time to pray out any changes that need to be made. You never want to make drastic changes without truly praying them through. Your heart needs to be settled before you move forward. Remember, we never want to simply ask God to bless what we are doing. We want to find out what He is doing and get on board with it! Besides, if we don't get God's heart on the matter no amount of good ideas will move our churches in the right direction.[145]

And while you're praying, **pray for wisdom.** Jesus' brother, James, wrote that God is generous with His wisdom.[146] I realize this book may be unsettling for some pastors and church leaders. It has taken us over 25 years of ministry to come to many of the conclusions in this book, and our understanding in this area is constantly growing. God is able to give you the wisdom you need to make the necessary changes, and the passion and courage to act on this knowledge.[147]

Invite Millennials to be a part of your team and to help you think through changes you need to make. (I'm assuming you have some in your church.) Ask them for honest feedback and then provide a safe place for them to disagree with you. They are the best guides to help you understand their generation. Make sure you differentiate between pushback and rebellion. It's okay for them to disagree with the strategy, but the God-given vision and core values are non-negotiable.

You do need to be open to their suggestions. They see the world through different glasses than you do, which means they also think differently than you do. If their insights and viewpoints are continually ignored or devalued they will typically either dropout or find another church. They want their voice to count. Unfortunately, their version of what a seasoned leader looks like – them – and your version – you – are quite different. You have to gently and patiently help them learn the importance of earning influence, especially with senior leaders.

Get an objective opinion. You may want to consider hiring an outside church consultant to give you an honest appraisal of your church or ministry. He/she should also be able to help you chart the course toward your desired destination. Make sure you do this BEFORE going public with your planned changes. Additionally, this consultant will help you cast the vision for change to your people. Your people will often have more confidence in your plan it if is endorsed by a professional church consultant.

Don't throw out the baby with the bath water. There are probably some positive traditions that have gotten the church this far. Affirm them and keep them, if you can. This provides a solid bridge to the changes you need to make. Besides, if it seems to your people that you are getting rid of everything they are used to and are starting over from scratch, they will be more likely to buck against your leadership.

Do the necessary diligence. Make sure you have a fully formed plan and a group of people that are *with you* before you announcing anything publicly. This was one mistake we made in Freiburg. We got no pushback from our staff on a change in strategy and assumed this meant they were with us. We were wrong.

It is important to get your key leaders in alignment concerning the planned changes. They don't necessarily have to be in agreement, but they do need to be aligned behind your plan and willing to support you. It's not necessary to have all your leaders on board, but most of them should be behind you before you move forward. I believe it is possible to turn a ship if you can get your early adopters in your corner, but you may need to be patient as they influence the rest of the team.

Choose your battles wisely. Some changes may need to be made right away. Many are better left for later, after you've earned more leadership clout. Other changes may need to wait until the church is at a place that it can financially or organizationally handle what you're asking your people to do. Some problems don't have to be dealt with at all. They will naturally work themselves out as your church grows in maturity. It's been said that the to get rid of sacred cows you need to either starve them or barbecue them. You need enough wisdom to know which solution is appropriate. Inviting a consultant or fellow pastor who can offer an objective point of view is often a wise move in helping you decide which changes to tackle, and in which order.

Never put the vision up for sale. There will be some that don't like the direction you are taking the church. They will attempt to manipulate you with their finances and influence, using phrases like, "I don't want my tithe going to that project," or, "If you do this, you won't get another dime from me." I know of a wealthy couple that told their pastor he was welcome make changes as long as he continued to do their pet program. "If not," they said, "this may not be our church any longer. We and all our friends will just leave!" Another said, "I hope you've got enough supporters to make your vision happen because I'm taking my money elsewhere." *(What's funny is that this man wasn't even a tither. And when he did give it wasn't very much.)*

When something like this happens I always quote Pastor Greg Surratt, "The vision is not for sale." If you confident you have God's vision for your church, hang onto it for dear life! Don't let anyone or anything distract you from it. On the other hand, you need to realize it may take a while to turn the ship.

Consider doing a trial period. At Watermark we introduced many changes with, "We have prayed about this and believe it is a God thing. We're going to try it for three months. If it doesn't work, we're not above admitting we made a mistake. We'll simply take it [the program] out back and shoot it. But let's at least give it our all so it has the best chance of success. Who knows? It might change everything!"

Sam Rainer says there are three possible decisions you can make at the end of your trial period: Extend the trial period, reverse the change or make the change permanent.[148] Don't allow internal or external pressure to make the decision for you. If you're not settled on an answer at the end of your stated trial period, extend the trial period and then reevaluate it.

Pace yourself. If you pastor an existing church or will be assuming leadership of one, don't try to change everything at once. A former colleague and wise friend, once told me, "People can only handle 10% change at any one time."[149] I didn't fully understand the implications then, but over the years I've realized that he was right. Changing the culture of an organization is a process that takes a lot of effort and patience, sort of like turning an ocean liner around.

Don't make sweeping changes without first getting your leaders and influencers on board. You'll need them on your side if you want to steer the ship in the right direction. You can turn the rudder, but without someone else adjusting the sails you will have a hard time reaching your destination. Give your people plenty of time to process what you're asking them to do. After all, change is often an emotional issue for most people, especially in an established church.

The pastor of a megachurch once said that at his church they never announce changes. They say they will be tweaking some things to make them better. Even if they were going to replace the entire staff, they would call it a tweak. In his words, "People can handle tweaks. They are freaked out by change."

Be sure to build enough credibility and influence before starting this process. It will require you to invest heavily in relationships with your key leaders and influencers.

Don't take opposition personally. People often lash out against change. Those that are willing to partner with you can help you enact the change. Those that don't are perfect candidates for prayer and patience.

Dr. Gerald Brooks says that in any given situation

- 10% of the people will be against whatever you do.

- 10% of the people will be for whatever you do.

- 80% aren't sure whether they are for or against you.

Simply understanding this fact will help you stay the course and maintain calm in the face of opposition.

Make sure your key influencers understand that they will be your first line of defense. People opposed to the changes you make will often passive-aggressively go to your key people (instead of coming to you, as the Bible requires) to complain about you. There *will* be pushback with any type of change in a church. Prepare your leaders by counting the cost with them.[150] In one of the churches we served, we didn't properly prepare our leaders for the pushback they would experience. Everyone suffered because of it.

If you *do* see the necessity of moving your church in this direction but realize you're not the one to lead your church into the future, you have a couple of options...

- **Church merger.** You could merge your church with another one, allowing them to absorb your members, facility and assets. Many churches are on life support, attempting to prolong the inevitable. They could be "organ donors" to a younger, life-giving church before they shut down completely. This could be a boost to the younger church and to yours. There are a number of great books on this subject.

- **Step aside.** You may come to the conclusion that you're not willing to make the necessary sacrifices or adjustments to take your church to the next level. Maybe you've grown comfortable or you're nearing retirement and want to play it safe. Or you may simply be too tired to lead your church into the future. For the sake of God's Church I beg you to prayerfully consider stepping aside and allowing someone else take the reins. After all, it's not *your* church. We are simply under-shepherds serving the Great Shepherd.[151] The Church is His Bride, and He expects us to give our all in fulfilling His dream for it.

This could take a few different forms... you could simply resign your position and walk away. Or you might remain at the church for a season and use your credibility with your people to help the next pastor enact the necessary changes. There is also the possibility of stepping into a supportive role, but this is usually difficult for someone who has sat in the first chair.

It will be difficult, no matter which road you choose. But the future of your church is worth it!

For Second Chair Leaders Or Others In Subordinate Positions

Realize that you're not in the driver's seat. If you're not sitting in the first chair, you have to use wisdom when trying to get those over you to implement changes. If you aren't the organizational leader you will have to earn the right to "lead upward."[152] You can't expect those over you – especially those with more experience – to automatically listen to you or allow you to influence the direction of the organization. Pressuring those over you to change without earning the necessary influence to ask for such a thing will actually hurt your credibility and diminish your influence in the long run.

The best way to earn credibility with those over you is to do your job well. The more you finish your tasks with excellence, with a positive attitude and in a timely manner, the more they will value your input. But if you give only satisfactory or substandard effort, don't expect to have a voice in the organization. Proverbs 22:29 reads, "Do you see a person skilled in his work? He will take his position before kings; he will not take his position before obscure people." If you want your voice to count, you'll need to develop your skills and be a consistently diligent worker. It often takes a frustratingly long time to develop influence – especially if you're serving an insecure leader – but it's well worth the effort.

Sow what you want to reap. The Law of the Farm states that we have to plant if we want to reap a harvest, and that we will only harvest what we've planted.[153] Plant good seed. Serve with your heart. Support your pastor and leaders with both your words and your attitude. Give it your full effort. Pray diligently for them. Be their greatest cheerleader. Honoring the people God sets over you will open doors of blessing you'll never see otherwise.

Be realistic. You have to decide if you can live with the current situation indefinitely. You have no guarantees that those over you will make the changes you desire, and it's not your place to demand that they do. They are the ones that have to answer to God for their decisions. If the status quo is unacceptable to you, you have two basic decisions:

- Stay and submit, praying for your leaders. This is the road less taken. Paul asked Timothy to stay in Ephesus so he could sort out some problems.[154] I'm sure it would have been much easier to leave. There were some major problems with that congregation. But they needed a leader to help them sort things out and provide stability. The times we've stayed at our post were very difficult, but proved to be times of HUGE growth in our spiritual lives.

- Leave and keep your mouth shut. Many leave. Few keep their mouths shut. Once we made the mistake of thinking we had to have a "word from God" before moving on. Although we experienced personal growth through the process, we created needless stress for ourselves, our pastors and our church by staying as long as we did. As we've already written, if the issue is causing you to not respect your pastor, you are usually better off leaving.

Thoughts On Transition

If and when you do decide it is time for you to move on, I have some advice for you. *How* **you leave one phase of life determines how successful you'll be in the next.** The way you leave (a place) is the same way you enter (the next one), so make sure you leave well. You don't want to bring emotional baggage with you into your next position, so make sure you finish this season well.

All of us have to face transitions. And since every transition is different, it's never easy. There is always a learning curve. Sometimes it's a transition of place, such as relocating from one town to another, or even moving to a new house. Maybe it's something as common as going to a new school or starting a new job. Other times it's emotionally painful – even devastating – such as the death of a loved one or a divorce.

Whatever the case may be, transitions are a normal part of life. We need to know how to handle them in order to make a clean break from the place we're leaving. We want to enter the next place with the right heart and attitude.

Here are some things I think we all need to remember about transitions:

First, I think it's important to **keep your life connected.** In other words, turn *to* God, not *from* Him. It's not His fault if things aren't going smoothly. He didn't cause your trouble, but He will use it for the greater good if you'll stay connected to Him. Psalm 46:1 reveals that God is a "very present help in trouble." You'll need His help to get through this unscathed. Walking toward Him counteracts burnout. Walking away from Him increases the feelings of isolation, loneliness and frustration.

Next, you need to remember to **keep your heart right.** Make sure your attitudes and actions are motivated by love. The Apostle Paul wrote, "Your attitude should be the same as that of Christ Jesus."[155] Sometimes in our desire to be right we lash out at others. This hurts both us and the target of our aggression.

You need to refuse to demonize either the people or the place you're leaving. We want everyone to know that *we* are right (a sign of insecurity), so we make sure everyone involved knows *our* side of the story. This attempt to put ourselves in a good light is often at the expense of another person. The problem is that it hurts everyone involved if you make the other person out to be the bad guy. *You can BOTH be right!* Keeping your heart and attitudes right counteracts frustration.

One thing we've learned through our transitions is that as your season in a place is coming to an end, the "grace" to serve there begins to wane. This grace acts like blinders, helping us to stay focused on the mission God gives us. But when the grace begins to lift it's as if the blinders are removed.

I think for many people when there is change ahead God begins by first moving their hearts, and then the rest of them. There seems to be a general feeling of *discontent* in this season. If we're not careful we begin to look at our surroundings, our job, our church or its leaders as the source of this *frustration*... when actually it is God's leading. It may feel as if our job or church has changed, when in reality everything remains the same. *We* are the ones who have changed.

It's often quite hard to do, but you need to **keep your mouth shut.** Never let a critical word leave your lips. Don't allow your words to cut off a possible future source of blessing. You don't want to have to reap when you sow like that!

Remember: It's hard to be critical of someone you're actively praying for. Peter wrote, "Do not repay evil with evil or insult with insult, but with blessing, because to this you were called so that you may inherit a blessing...."[156] Our tendency is to try to get people "on our side." We may not call it such, but in the final analysis we simply want to be vindicated. God's antidote for this selfish desire is to pray for and speak a blessing over those that frustrate us.

You should always **keep your bridges intact.** Keep relationships open as much as it is possible with you. It may not be possible to restore some relationships. Too much damage may have been done, or the other person may not be willing to restore the relationship.

If that is the case, let them know that you love them and will be praying for them. Apologize for any hurt you may have caused... even if it makes you vulnerable to their attacks.

Matthew 5:23-24 and Mark 18:15 make it abundantly clear that it is *my* responsibility to keep relationships open, no matter *who* is at fault. In these verses we are instructed to forgive anything we have against others and make the first step toward others that have something against us.

And finally, **keep your mind and heart in the game.** Give your very best until the day your transition is completed. Leave things better than they were when you came. Then you can set out on your new adventure without any feelings of guilt. This is quite hard when you are sensing a disconnection in your heart, but it is absolutely necessary. Even through His suffering while dying on the cross Jesus kept His mind and heart in the game enough to make room for one more "sinner."[157]

Transitions are never easy. There is always a cost involved. Sometimes there are even "hidden fees" that we didn't expect. But regardless of our circumstances, we can intentionally choose our response. If you choose to do the above things, you'll see a rich payoff on the other side of the transition.

If you are sensing a transition is at hand, the most important thing to do is take time to seek God's will. You need to know for sure if you're supposed to stay or if it's time to leave. And be sure to seek the counsel of a spiritually mature, uninvolved third party. This only works if you're honest with them, not simply painting yourself in the best possible light or putting your spin on the situation.

Some people leave too soon; others too late. Both of these cause pain to everyone involved. Knowing God's will in the matter gives you much needed confidence to follow through on the decision you know you need to make. However, if your presence there is continually causing strife, it's better for you and for the organization that you leave.

Chapter 24
Finish Strong

As I write this I'm sitting out on the deck of a small cabin at a Christian camp in Comfort, Texas. There's a heavy fog hanging over the valley, much like what we experienced in the Black Forest of Germany. It has left the spider webs on the trees in front of me wet with dew. As they blow in the breeze I can see that at least one spider has been quite industrious overnight. It takes time to build a good web. It doesn't happen instantly. Unfortunately for the spider, animals, humans, weather and other natural forces can in one moment destroy the web it worked so hard to build.

One thing I've noticed about spiders is that when their webs are destroyed they get right back to work building another one. Regrettably, humans aren't usually so resilient. We get our feelings hurt and throw a pity party. We call our friends and commiserate about how hard ministry is. We ask God why He has abandoned us. Many simply shut down. Dr. Gerald Brooks says that our ministries will grow to the size of our pain threshold. When the price gets too high we just quit pushing forward.

But what would happen if we had the tenacity of a spider? If every time someone messed up what we had so meticulously planned, or said something hurtful about us, or questioned our motives, or intentionally tried to sabotage what we've worked so hard to build – what would happen if instead of shutting down we prayed, courageously got back up, dusted ourselves off and started building again? What would we, by the grace of God, be able to achieve in our lifetime?

Don't Throw In The Towel

We are all given marvelous opportunities to quit. The big question is: Will we succumb? Unfortunately the odds are against us:

- 1,000 new churches begin each year while 4,000 churches close.

- Fifteen hundred pastors leave the ministry each month due to moral failure, spiritual burnout, or contention in their churches.

- Eighty percent of seminary and Bible school graduates who enter the ministry will leave the ministry within the first five years.[158]

These stats are not encouraging. They tell us that not only are pastors walking away, but what's worse, there aren't enough young pastors waiting in the wings to replace them.

Many years ago Dr. Lester Sumrall was in a minister's meeting and was asked how he was able to build such a large ministry (radio/shortwave stations throughout the world, feed the hungry program, ministering to world leaders, etc.)… how had he been able to accomplish so much in his lifetime. He thought about it for a minute and answered, "I just didn't quit."

I believe this is the key to success for spiritual leaders. And it is my challenge to you. Don't quit! Maybe you've been hurt, lied about, deceived or betrayed. Maybe you've labored with all your heart only to see what you've built come crashing down, or had someone else usurp your leadership position. Maybe you were asked to abdicate your leadership position after serving for a long time. But now's not the time to back off or give up. Now is the time to get back in the game, seek God wholeheartedly and take new steps of faith. Serving God seems risky, but the payoff is huge!

Let me encourage pastors and spiritual leaders reading this book. If you are debating leaving the ministry, don't make a decision yet. Take some more time to pray it through first. Find a place to get quiet and seek God. More than likely if you've read this far you really *do* want to revitalize your church or take it to the next level. Ministry is tough, and very few of the people around you can understand the pressure you face on a regular basis.

But they also can't grasp the "call" on your life. Do you remember back to when God first spoke to you about being in ministry? Can you recall the passion that came with that call? Look at what the Apostle Paul wrote to the church at Ephesus:

> *God has made us what we are. In Christ Jesus, God made us to do good works, which God planned in advance for us to live our lives doing.*

Ephesians 2:10 ERV

God has created us on purpose and for a purpose. He has given us the necessary gifts and talents to accomplish everything He's called us to do. If there is a call on your life, God expects you to fulfill it. He knew what He was doing when He created you, and when He called you to serve Him in the ministry. And you responded, trusting that He knew what He was doing.

Yes, much has happened since then. But what about the call? Don't God and His will get a vote when it comes to us shutting down and throwing in the towel? God has given you a responsibility. If you fail to finish your race there will be a gaping hole in His plan. Yes, the overarching will of God will come to pass. But the world won't get an accurate picture of who God is if we don't get into position. It's sort of like a puzzle. When a few of the pieces are missing the picture doesn't look like it should.

It's Your Choice

Your history up to this point doesn't matter. It's not important how badly you failed or messed up. What counts is that you finish strong. People won't remember how you started, but rather how you finish. The Bible is full of people that messed up and yet still finished well. I believe one of the best examples is John Mark.

In Acts 13 we find Paul and Barnabas preparing to head out on their first mission trip, empowered and cheered on by the megachurch in Jerusalem and "sent out by the Holy Spirit."

They chose a young leader named John Mark to go with them. He was probably just like many of us were (or are) – full of passion and talent, ready to jump headfirst into the deep water of ministry. "No stopping us now… we're headed out into the world to fulfill our destiny!"

Although Scripture doesn't give us a reason why, it is clear that John Mark abandoned the mission when they were getting ready to head deeper into Asia Minor (present-day Turkey). It could be that their encounter with Elymas the sorcerer shook him. Or possibly that Paul's choleric Type A, "my way or the highway" personality was too much to handle on a daily basis.

Think of how John Mark must have felt returning home after abandoning the mission trip. The church was excited to see him head out on mission. Now they must have felt a sense of disappointment. I'm sure there was a measure of gossip and whispering about him as well. He probably felt as if he had let them down. He most certainly felt shame and humiliation. This was a high profile failure. It's hard to recover from something like that.

Thankfully God provided someone to mentor him. Barnabas (whose name means "Son of Encouragement") believed in the call on John Mark's life, and he was willing to go toe to toe with Paul in defending him. The argument became so great that Paul and Barnabas each went their separate ways and chose new partners. And although it appeared that this amazing team had just split up, now there were two teams headed out to do the work of spreading the Message!

The narrative in the Book of Acts follows Paul's life, not Barnabas'. Because of this we don't have any details as to what happened next. We don't get to see the encouragement and accountability that Barnabas brought to John Mark. Until we get to heaven we'll never know what Barnabas' debrief of John Mark's failure looked like.

What we do know is that many years later, as Paul's life and ministry were coming to a close, he wrote from prison to Timothy, his protégé. He asked him to bring John Mark with him when he came to visit. In Paul's words, "He will be helpful to me in my ministry."[159] What a comeback! This is the same guy that Paul refused to take with him.

Here's the lesson we need to learn. Failure doesn't have to be fatal, futile or final. If you've been knocked down, it's your choice whether to stay down or to get back up and fight. You can learn from your failure, and then pass on that knowledge to the next generation. You get to decide what your future will look like. It is a blank page... You and God hold the pen. Write whatever you want. Don't give your past a vote.

Paul understood this point and wrote these words: "God began a good work in you, and I am sure he will continue it until it is finished when Jesus Christ comes again."[160] I believe the same about you... God got you started on this journey. He will help you complete it.

Get back in the game! Find a mentor or a counselor. Find a small group where you can be yourself and let your guard down. It's difficult to find a place to be authentic and unload all your stuff, but it's crucial to the long-term success of the destiny God has prepared for you! Even Jesus had a close circle of friends to do life with.

If you don't know where to begin, follow the advice you would give someone else in your shoes: Start doing those things that you *do* know to do (spiritual disciplines), even when you don't feel like it. Scientists have proven that you're more likely to act your way into feeling than you are to feel your way into acting.

We need you to finish strong. The stakes couldn't be higher! God is counting on you. A world that is rapidly self-destructing needs what you have to offer. And the rest of us in ministry need you to take your place! Together we can meet all the challenges that Post-Christianity throws at us.

A Final Word
At the end of the day we are only responsible to do our part. The Apostle Paul understood this plainly when he wrote, "I planted the seed, Apollos watered it, but God has been making it grow."[161] God has called us to do our very best to

reach those far from Him, and to disciple them into a growing relationship with Him. We can't force people to come in, just as we can't force our churches to grow.

But to use the excuses, "What we're doing is working just fine," or "We tried that before, but it didn't work," is a cop-out that will keep our churches from becoming what they were intended to be. When leaders fail to look to the horizon to see what is coming they are inevitably headed for a crash. We're approaching the edge of a cliff and we need to make some adjustments.

I know the task ahead of us seems daunting. You can easily feel overwhelmed. But thankfully God hasn't left us alone to deal with things. The Holy Spirit is here to work with us and help us accomplish God's plan. Never forget that He knows what He's doing. He knew everything about you when He called you. He believes you are well able (by cooperating with Him) to fulfill your destiny.

Fifty percent of the people in ministry today will "tap out" in the next 10 years.[162] The Church can't afford to take a hit like this. If you bail out, someone else will have to pay the price you've already paid and learn the lessons you've already learned. We don't have time for this. There's too much at stake! There are not enough seasoned leaders on the team roster for us to abandon our posts. If we quit or fail, the mission of the Church will be hindered. I don't want to stand before my Father with little or nothing to show for my life.

These lessons you learned weren't in vain, unless you throw in the towel. Politicians will tell you that we should never waste a good crisis. They always want to use it to manipulate and control the population.

Your Father never wastes a crisis either. He doesn't cause them, and He certainly doesn't use them to manipulate or "guide" us. He does, however, use them for our good.[163] The Apostle Paul had learned this. That is why from a first century jail cell he wrote the following words:

> *Christian brothers, I want you to know that what has happened to me has helped spread the Good News... Because of*

your prayers and the help the Holy Spirit gives me, all of this will turn out for good.

Philippians 1:12, 19 NLV

God is able to use the ugly, painful situations that you've experienced... but only if you let Him. If you hold onto the hurt, the disappointment, the pain and the grief you'll never experience the grace, mercy and comfort that He so readily provides. Turn TO Him and not AWAY from Him.

You need to know that Robin and I are praying for you. The Church needs you to keep your heart and your mind focused on the heart of God and what he would say to you. Don't give up. As long as Jesus is alive there is hope for a better tomorrow. The best is yet to come!

Discussion Questions:

Make a list of changes that need to be made in your church or organization. Now prioritize them, putting a 1, 2, 3, etc. next to each one.

How will you enact these changes without overwhelming your people?

What are your intentional next steps? How will you bring others along with you on this journey?

Appendix

Our Websites:

PostChristianTsunami.com   (postchristiantsunami.com) –
The companion website to this book.   It was created to
continue the conversation on Post-Christianity, the unchurched
and future generations. It contains church evaluation tools and
a blog about leadership and ministry in a Post-Christian
context.

Perrin Ministries Online (perrinministries.org) – A blog and
other materials on leadership, ministry, spiritual formation and
cultural trends, as well as Bible studies, Bible Discussion Guides
(a one-year Bible study curriculum designed to get your small
group talking), leadership mp3s and more (in multiple
languages).

Church Planting Blog (watermarkfreiburg.blogspot.com) – I
tried   as   much   as   possible   to   journal   my   major
thoughts/experiences during the first two years of our church
planting journey in Post-Christian Freiburg, Germany.

Other Useful Websites:

GeraldBrooksMinistries.com

AndyStanley.com

CareyNieuwhof.com

TonyMorganLive.com

RonEdmonson.com

PerryNoble.com

CraigGroeschel.com

MackLakeOnline.com

JohnMaxwell.com

BillHybels.com

DanReiland.com

SethGodin.com

Barna.org

Open.church

Recommended Books:

The following books have helped in our leadership journey.

Deep & Wide (Andy Stanley)

Visioneering (Andy Stanley)

Courageous Leadership (Bill Hybels)

Up The Middle Church (Matt Keller)

Zero To Sixty (Bob Franquiz)

Good to Great (Jim Collins)

The E-Myth Revisited (Michael E. Gerber)

The Leisure Suit series (Tony Morgan)

Ready, Set, Grow (Scott Wilson)

Church Unique (Will Mancini)

Understanding Your Pain Threshhold (Dr. Gerald Brooks)

The Blessed Church (Robert Morris)

Purple Cow (Seth Godin)

Lasting Impact (Carey Nieuwhof)

The Five Dysfunctions Of A Team (Patrick Lencioni)

All of Dr. John C. Maxwell's books

Conferences / Training Resources:

Gerald Brooks Ministries / North Texas Leadership Conference (geraldbrooksministries.com)

Global Leadership Summit / Willow Creek Community Church (www.willowcreek.com/events/leadership)

Auxano / Church Unique (auxano.com)

The Orange Conference / ReThink Leadership (rethinkleadership.com)

ARC church planting network (arcchurches.com)

The Nines (thenines.tv)

ABOUT THE AUTHOR

Jon Perrin brings over 25 years of ministry experience to the table. After resigning his Associate Pastor position in a mega-church, Jon and his wife, Robin moved their young family to Germany in 2001 (three weeks after 9/11). There they focused on empowering European church leaders through mentoring and coaching, as well as teaching in seminars, conferences and Bible Schools. They also helped plant a number of churches and youth groups throughout central Europe. They planted and pastored a highly successful "church for those who don't do church" in Freiburg, Germany.

After handing over their church, they returned to Texas in 2014 to help US churches prepare for the coming Post-Christian cultural shift. Although he resides in scenic Boerne, TX, Jon continues to equip Christian leaders throughout Europe and North America through consulting and coaching / mentoring, and through his online presence: perrinministries.org. Jon continues to empower leaders and mobilize churches to reach the unchurched.

Jon and Robin have been married since 1993 and have three children: Ryan, Ashton and Emma.

BIBLIOGRAPHY

[1] Szczepanski, Kellie. "2004 Indian Ocean Tsunami History and Aftermath." *About.com*. N.p., n.d. Web. 10 Feb. 2015. <http://asianhistory.about.com/od/asianenvironmentalhistory/p/The-2004-Tsunami-In-The-Indian-Ocean.htm>.

[2] Wikipedia. "2004 Indian Ocean Earthquake And Tsunami." *Wikipedia*. N.p., n.d. Web. N.p., n.d. Web. 10 Feb. 2015. <https://en.wikipedia.org/wiki/2004_Indian_Ocean_earthquake_and_tsunami#Humanitarian.2C_economic_and_environmental_impact>

[3] Pickrell, John. "Facts and Figures: Asian Tsunami Disaster." *The New Scientist*. N.p., 20 Jan. 2015. Web. 10 Feb. 2015. <http://www.newscientist.com/article/dn9931-facts-and-figures-asian-tsunami-disaster.html>.

[4] Wikipedia "2004 Indian Ocean Earthquake And Tsunami."

[5] About.com "2004 Indian Ocean Tsunami History and Aftermath."

[6] Acts 8:1-4

[7] Mark 16:15

[8] Matthew 9:9-12

[9] Luke 15:1-2

[10] Luke 19:10

[11] Psalm 127:1

[12] Matthew 5:13-16

[13] The Perrin Ministries Leadership Blog can be found at: http://perrinministries.org.

[14] Psalm 127:1

[15] Barna Research Group. "Millennials and the Bible: 3 Surprising Insights." *Barna.org*. N.p., n.d. Web. 10 Nov. 2014

<https://www.barna.org/barna-update/millennials/687-millennials-and-the-bible-3-surprising-insights>

[16] Matthew 5:14-16

[17] John 1:5

[18] 2 Corinthians 6:17

[19] Judges 17:6, 21:25

[20] Barna Research Group. "How Post-Christian Is America?" *Barna.org.* N.p., 15 Apr. 2013. Web. 28 Dec. 2014. <https://www.barna.org/barna-update/culture/608-hpca>.

[21] Sanchez, Daniel Raul. *Church Planting Movements in North America.* Fort Worth, TX: Church Starting Network, 2006. Print.

[22] McDonald, Mark. "Church Decline: Would Anyone Notice If Your Church Disappeared?" *Church Marketing Sucks.* N.p., 6 Oct. 2014. Web. 3 Jan. 2015. <http://www.churchmarketingsucks.com/2014/10/church-decline/>.

[23] Stetzer, Ed. "The Real Reason Why Young Adults Drop Out Of Church." *The Exchange.* N.p., 1 Dec. 2014. Web. 1 Dec. 2014. <http://www.christianitytoday.com/edstetzer/2014/december/real-reasons-young-adults-drop-out-of-church.html>

[24] Nieuwhof, Carey. "CNLP 004: Why Young Adults Are Walking Away from the Church & What You Can Do About It—An Interview with Kara Powell", *Carey Nieuwhof Leadership Podcast.* N.p., 7 Oct. 2014. Web. 7 Oct. 2014. <http://careynieuwhof.com/2014/10/episode4/>

[25] Barna Research Group. "Three Spiritual Journeys of Millennials." *Barna.org.* N.p., 9 May 2013. Web. 9 Nov. 2014. <https://www.barna.org/barna-update/teens-nextgen/612-three-spiritual-journeys-of-millennials/>

[26] SDA 4.0. "Selected Study:GSS 1972-2012 Cumulative Datafile." *SDA 4.0.* N.p., n.d. Web. 3 Jan. 2015.

<http://sda.berkeley.edu/sdaweb/analysis/?dataset=gss12>

[27] Public Religion Research Institute. "I Know What You Did Last Sunday." *Public Religion Research Institute*. N.p., 17 May 2014. Web. 24 Nov. 2014 <http://publicreligion.org/site/wp-content/uploads/2014/05/AAPOR-2014-Final.pdf>

[28] Pew Research Center. "'Nones' On The Rise." *PewResearch Religion & Public Life Project*. N.p., 9 Oct. 2012. Web. 28 Dec. 2014. <http://www.pewforum.org/2012/10/09/nones-on-the-rise/>

[29] Pastors.com. "Measuring Post-Christianity: How Will It Impact Your Ministry?." *Pastors.com*. N.p., 17 Apr. 2013. Web. 29.Apr. 2013. <http://pastors.com/measuring-post-christianity-how-will-it-impact-your-ministry>

[30] Rainer, Thomas S. "Five Reasons Why Millennials Do Not Want to Be Pastors or Staff in Established Churches." *ChurchLeaders.com*. N.p., n.d. Web. 12 Dec. 2014. <http://www.churchleaders.com/pastors/pastor-articles/243639-five-reasons-millennials-not-want-pastors-staff-established-churches.html>

[31] Luke 15:12

[32] Gupta, Nisha "The Saatchi Y-Spot: Slash/Slash." *Hudson/Houston* N.p., 11 Jun. 2010. Web. 8 Oct. 2014. <http://www.hudsonhouston.com/2010/06/the-saatchi-y-spot-slashslash/>

[33] Komando, Kim. "5 ways the workplace will change in 5 years." *Komando.com*. N.p., 8 Oct. 2014. Web. 8 Oct. 2014 <http://www.komando.com/small-business/275119/5-ways-the-workplace-will-change-in-5-years/>

[34] Komando "5 ways the workplace will change in 5 years."

[35] Thumma, Scott. "A Report on the 2010 National Profile of U.S. Nondenominational and Independent Churches." *Hartford Institute of Religion Research*. N.p., n.d. Web. 28 Dec. 2014. <http://www.hartfordinstitute.org/cong/nondenominational-churches-national-profile-2010.html>

[36] Barna Group. "Millennials and the Bible: 3 Surprising Insights." *Barna Group.* N.p., n.d. Web. 10 Nov. 2014. <https://www.barna.org/barna-update/millennials/687-millennials-and-the-bible-3-surprising-insights/>

[37] Evans, Rachel Held. "Why Millenials Are Leaving The Church." *CNN Belief Blog.* Cable News Network. Turner Broadcasting System, Inc., 27 Jul. 2013. Web. 20 Aug. 2014. <http://religion.blogs.cnn.com/2013/07/27/why-millennials-are-leaving-the-church/>

[38] Barna.org. "Six Reasons Young Christians Leave Church." *Barna Group.* N.p., 28 Sep. 2011. Web. 15 Oct. 2014. <https://www.barna.org/barna-update/millennials/528-six-reasons-young-christians-leave-church>

[39] Barna.org "Six Reasons Young Christians Leave Church."

[40] Isaiah 42:1, 60:3

[41] Matthew 6:4

[42] Matthew 28:18-20

[43] Psalm 23

[44] Revelation 21:4

[45] Matthew 7:1

[46] Rainer, Thomas S. "Top Ten Ways Churches Drive Away First-time Guests." ThomRainer.com. LifeWay Christian Resources, 1 Nov. 2014. Web. 1 Nov. 2014. <http://thomrainer.com/2014/11/01/top-ten-ways-churches-drive-away-first-time-guests/>

[47] Rainer, Thomas S. "Should Your Church Stop Having a Stand and Greet Time?" ThomRainer.com. LifeWay Christian Resources, 3 Nov. 2014. Web. 3 Nov. 2014. <http://thomrainer.com/2014/11/03/church-stop-stand-greet-time/>

[48] John 11:1-44

[49] Dr. Gerald Brooks.

[50] Matthew 7:29 MSG

[51] Proverbs 18:21

[52] Mark 11:23, 2 Corinthians 4:13

[53] 1 Corinthians 10:11

[54] 1 Samuel 20:1

[55] Acts 4:23-31

[56] 2 Corinthians 1:8-9

[57] Matthew 26:38

[58] Psalm 23

[59] Matthew 5:16 MSG

[60] http://postchristiantsunami.com/blog/

[61] Wilson, Scott. Ready, Set Grow: Three Conversations That Will Bring Lasting Growth to Your Church. Springfield, MO: My Healthy Church, 2013. Kindle Edition.

[62] Wilson "Ready, Set Grow: Three Conversations That Will Bring Lasting Growth to Your Church."

[63] Luke 14:28-30

[64] Luke 19:10

[65] Mark 16:15

[66] Matthew 5:14

[67] Ephesians 2:12

[68] 2 Corinthians 5:18-20

[69] The Perrin Ministries Leadership Blog can be found at: http://perrinministries.org.

[70] Mark 9:23

[71] The Perrin Ministries Leadership Blog can be found at: http://perrinministries.org.

[72] Morgan, Tony. "Would you rather?: 10 Competing Choices for Growing Churches." *TonyMorganLive.com.* N.p., 24.Oct.

2014. Web. 24 Oct. 2014. <http://tonymorganlive.com/2014/10/27/rather-10-choices-growing-churches-make/>

[73]Kawasaki, Guy. "Behind the scenes of Disney--how leadership and innovation make the magic happen." *American Express OPEN forum*. N.p., N.d. Web. 6 Jan. 2015. <https://www.americanexpress.com/us/small-business/openforum/articles/what-i-learned-from-a-mouse-with-big-ears/>

[74] Romans 5:8

[75] John 4

[76] John 8:1-11

[77] Luke 19:1-10

[78] John 21

[79] 1 Corinthians 5:12

[80] Colossians 2:20-3:4

[81] Ephesians 4:29

[82] Spurgeon, Charles. *The Soul Winner*. N.p.: Passmore & Alabaster, 1903. Print.

[83] 1 Corinthians 9:24-27

[84] 2 Timothy 4:6-8

[85] 1 Corinthians 9:7

[86] Titus 1:12

[87] The Greek word Jesus used that is translated as "Hypocrites" refers to thespians, literally: "play actors."

[88] Luke 20:24-25

[89] Luke 13:1-3

[90] Barna.org. "Millennials and the Bible: 3 Surprising Insights." Barna.org. N.p., 14 Oct. 2014. Web. 1 Nov. 2014. <https://www.barna.org/barna-update/millennials/687-

millennials-and-the-bible-3-surprising-insights/>

[91] Springle, Pat. *Communicating With The Postmodern Culture*. N.p.: Leadership Network, 2007. 5. Print.

[92] Barna.org. "What People Experience In Churches." *Barna.org.* N.p., 9 Jan. 2012. Web. 1 Dec. 2014. <https://www.barna.org/barna-update/congregations/556-what-people-experience-in-churches>

[93] Ephesians 4:11-13

[94] John 15:13

[95] Mark 8:27-29

[96] Wilson "Ready, Set Grow: Three Conversations That Will Bring Lasting Growth to Your Church."

[97] Mark 5:21-34

[98] Dr. Gerald Brooks.

[99] Luke 15:4

[100] Pastor Randy Ayers of Cross Mountain Church in San Antonio, TX.

[101] Carey Nieuwhof. "CNLP 012: Strategic Leadership Lessons From Disney – An Interview with Steven Barr." *CareyNieuwhof.com.* N.p., 2 Dec. 2014. Web. 2 Dec. 2014. <http://careynieuwhof.com/2014/12/episode12/>

[102] Dr. Gerald Brooks.

[103] Graham, Casey. "CNLP 003: The Best Practices Church Leaders Can Adopt from Business Leaders & Vice-Versa — An Interview with Casey Graham." *CareyNieuwhof Leadership Podcast.* N.p., 30 Sep. 2014. Web. 10 Oct. 2014. <http://careynieuwhof.com/2014/09/episode3/>

[104] Mark 3:14

[105] Luke 10:1

[106] Mark 5:37, 9:2, 14:33

[107] Matthew 14:22-33

[108] Nieuwhof, Carey. "How to Ruin the Chances of Change Happening in Your Church (In One Simple Step)." *CareyNieuwhof.com*. N.p., 6 Mar. 2014. Web. 12 May. 2014. <http://careynieuwhof.com/2014/03/how-to-ruin-the-chances-of-change-happening-in-your-church-in-one-simple-step/>

[109] Dr. Gerald Brooks.

[110] Dr. Gerald Brooks.

[111] Galatians 6:7-10

[112] Dr. Gerald Brooks.

[113] Acts 13:36

[114] Read Proverbs chapters 1 - 10.

[115] Collins, James C. Good to Great: Why Some Companies Make the Leap ... and Others Don't. New York, NY: HarperBusiness, 2001. Print.

[116] 1 Timothy 2:4

[117] 2 Peter 3:9

[118] Proverbs 31:8

[119] Genesis 1:26

[120] Rainer, Thomas S. "Facts & Trends, "Seven Common Comments Non-Christians Make about Christians." *Facts & Trends*. LifeWay Christian Resources, 7 Feb. 2013. Web. 30 Dec. 2014., <http://factsandtrends.net/2013/02/07/seven-common-comments-non-christians-make-about-christians/>

[121] Luke 10:5-7

[122] John 4

[123] For more information see http://servolution.org.

[124] Acts 2:42-47

[125] Genesis 2:18

[126] Genesis 2:18

[127] Discovery.com. "Britain's 'Atheist Church' Set to Go Global." *Discovery.com news*. AFP, 8 Mar. 2013. Web. 11 Nov. 2014. <http://news.discovery.com/human/life/atheist-church-set-to-go-global-130308.htm>

[128] Nieuwhof, Carey. "The Impending Death (and Rebirth) of Cool Church." *CareyNieuwhof.com*. N.p., 19 Dec. 2014. Web. 27 Dec. 2014. <http://careynieuwhof.com/2014/12/impending-death-rebirth-cool-church/>

[129] John 13:34-35

[130] John 15:5

[131] Psalm 46:10

[132] Ephesians 5:2

[133] Philip Woods, Spiritual Growth Pastor at Cross Mountain Church in Boerne, TX.

[134] Dr. Gerald Brooks.

[135] Mark 2:15-16

[136] Matthew 20:20

[137] White, Allen. "The Hard Work of Getting Along." *Galatians419*. N.p., 26 Sep. 2011. Web. 18 Dec. 2014. <http://galatians419.blogspot.com/2011/09/hard-work-of-getting-along.html>

[138] Mark 10:41

[139] Luke 9:54

[140] Luke 9:46

[141] Matthew 26:75

[142] Matthew 8:25, John 20:19

[143] Matthew 14:31

[144] John 20:20

[145] Psalm 127:1

[146] James 1:5

[147] Philippians 2:13

[148] Rainer, Sam. "Twelve Principles For Change In The Established Church." SamRainer.com. N.p., 28 Dec. 2014. Web. 28 Dec. 2014. <http://samrainer.com/2014/12/twelve-principles-for-change-in-the-established-church/>

[149] Dr. Deane Parker.

[150] Luke 14:28

[151] 1 Peter 5:1-4

[152] John Maxwell's book "The 360° Leader" talks about this process.

[153] Galatians 6:7-9

[154] 1 Timothy 1:3

[155] Philippians 2:5

[156] 1 Peter 3:9

[157] Luke 23:43

[158] Pastoral Care Inc. "Statistics in the Ministry." *Pastoral Care Inc.* N.p., N.d. Web. 7 Jan. 2015. <http://www.pastoralcareinc.com/statistics/>

[159] 2 Timothy 4:11

[160] Philippians 1:6

[161] 1 Corinthians 3:6

[162] Pastoral Care Inc. "Statistics in the Ministry."

[163] Romans 8:28, Genesis 50:20